Praise for *Your Killer Emotions*

D1009360

"Ken Lindner's phenomenal book, *Your Killer Emotions*, puts you in the driver's seat of your life! It enlightens, empowers and provides an essential foundation for achieving success, health, well-being, and fulfillment. It provides, in a clear and compelling way, a true, *essential life compass* that directs and motivates you to manage negative, self-destructive, and self-defeating behavior and to redirect your emotions in a way that harnesses a positive and strategic force. Lindner's book opens the door to this positive emotional force and gives you the tools you need to help keep you on track and allow your greatest talents, skills, and aspirations to flourish, and for you to succeed in the areas you value most!"

—Don Browne, former president of
Telemundo Communications Group; executive vice president,
NBC News; and member of the Broadcasting Hall of Fame

"If you are looking for a clear, commonsense, and effective way to improve your life, look no further! *Your Killer Emotions* is a phenomenally unique book that takes an in-depth look at the way we make decisions, while illustrating the importance of the emotional milieu behind these decisions via a series of personal and professional stories. Reading this book will change the way you understand your emotions and empower you to control and actually use your emotional "energy charges" to create the life you really want. Ken Lindner has provided us with a true game-changer. Caution—reading this book may drastically improve your life!"

—Natalie Strand, MD

"If you read *Your Killer Emotions*, you will be far more effective at what you do, more successful, and most importantly—you will be happier!"

—Sanjay Gupta, MD, multiple Emmy®-award-winning
chief medical correspondent for CNN

"No more excuses that you can't control your life, your emotions, and your choices because of raging hormones, past experiences, or lack of willpower! *Your Killer Emotions* provides practical tools, techniques, and tips to live consciously, gratefully, gracefully, and with intention."

—Lois P. Frankel, PhD, author of
Nice Girls Don't Get the Corner Office and *Stop Sabotaging Your Career*

"I love this book! It is a great tool for all of us. In our everyday lives, all of us deal with a range of complex issues and challenging emotional choices that are impactful to our journeys. In Ken Lindner's *Your Killer Emotions*, he presents a compendium of vignettes leading to comprehensive and systematic prescriptions for making real-life decisions. With the meticulousness of a surgeon, Lindner creates tried and true therapeutic interventions for the emotionally confused, disabled, and compromised. This is a must-read! Armed with this new tool box of techniques and protocols, the reader can better meet the challenges that life brings."

—Bert R. Mandelbaum, MD, DHL,
physician for the U.S. Olympic Soccer Team

"*Your Killer Emotions* gives the reader specific tools to work through stored emotions that can unknowingly move our lives in a very negative direction, while not understanding why. This book is not just for those who have found themselves accepting a less than desirable relationship, job, or life situation; it is also for those doing well, but, with a desire to do even better. Having worked in the medical field for over twenty-five years, I have seen the negative impact of stored emotions in the lives of my patients. This book not only helps us understand how our beliefs, perceptions, and attitudes about life can impact our decision making, it provides a way to move beyond the negative impact of our old emotions. While working with a mountain rescue team, I learned that, if lost, I should find the highest peak in order to gain the best possible perspective to find my way out. Ken Lindner's book is this peak."

—Dr. Douglas Krech

"I thoroughly enjoyed Ken Lindner's *Your Killer Emotions*. This book is an instant classic! The affective (emotional) realm is largely unexplored in self-help books. We all need to pause, respond to life, and act based upon our core values. With so many stressors in our lives, getting control of our emotions is more critical than ever before. With this in mind, *Your Killer Emotions* should be required reading for everyone!"

—**Steve Cohen, news director, KUSI-TV**

"In *Your Killer Emotions*, Ken Lindner provides a masterful blueprint for overcoming the emotional obstacles that block the path to achieving the personal success we all hope for but find so elusive. *Your Killer Emotions* offers a truly effective how-to guide to tame, and even harness, our deepest and most destructive emotions as a means to make our unique life experience be the very thing that helps us realize our dreams."

—**Cyndi Sarnoff-Ross, marriage and family therapist**

"*Your Killer Emotions* gives you a step-by-step guide to managing your emotions during life's challenging times. As a high school guidance counselor, I have already used 'The 7 Steps of Emotion Mastery' to help an adolescent de-escalate his toxic emotions for a powerfully positive outcome. Not only can you use 'The Steps' in your life, but they can be effectively applied to the lives of your children."

—**Joseph Havens, high school guidance counselor; BA, Harvard University; MBA, Amos Tuck, School of Business, Dartmouth College; teaching credential from the University of Irvine.**

"*Your Killer Emotions* equips you with a unique process that gives you the POWER to no longer make destructive, self-sabotaging life choices, but instead to make highly positive ones. I have no doubt that the advice and specific tips in *Your Killer Emotions* can improve your personal, social, and professional life. Take it to heart—it will change your life!"

—**Dr. Bruce Hensel, chief medical, health & science editor & correspondent, KNBC, and nine-time Emmy®-award winner**

The *NEW,*
Groundbreaking Process
for Mastering Your
Emotions and Modifying
Your Behavior

YOUR

KILLER

EMOTIONS

The **7** Steps to Mastering the Toxic Emotions,
Urges, and Impulses That Sabotage You

KEN LINDNER

THE FOUNDER OF *LIFE-CHOICE PSYCHOLOGY*™

GREENLEAF
BOOK GROUP PRESS

Some of the stories, cases, and examples in this book have been fictionalized and altered in order to protect the privacy of the individuals and their families. Please note that the stories, cases, and examples discussed in this book are solely meant to poignantly and memorably illustrate the *Steps*, strategies, and insights presented herein and are not meant to portray any particular person. Persons referenced in this book may be composites or entirely fictitious; thus, references to any real persons, living or dead, are not implied.

Published by Greenleaf Book Group Press
Austin, Texas
www.gbgpress.com

Distributed by Greenleaf Book Group LLC

For ordering information, please contact Greenleaf Book Group LLC at PO Box 91869, Austin, TX 78709, 512.891.6100.

Design and composition by Greenleaf Book Group LLC
Cover design by Greenleaf Book Group LLC

Publisher's Cataloging-In-Publication Data
(Prepared by The Donohue Group, Inc.)
Lindner, Ken.
    Your killer emotions : the 7 steps to mastering the toxic emotions, urges, and impulses that sabotage you /
Ken Lindner.—1st ed.
    p. ; cm.
    "The new, groundbreaking process for mastering your emotions and modifying your behavior."
    Issued also as an ebook.
    ISBN: 978-1-60832-380-7
    1. Self-control. 2. Emotions. 3. Decision making. 4. Conduct of life. I. Title.
BF632 .L56 2013
153.8   2012934888

Part of the Tree Neutral® program, which offsets the number of trees consumed in the production and printing of this book by taking proactive steps, such as planting trees in direct proportion to the number of trees used: www.treeneutral.com

TreeNeutral®

Printed in the United States of America on acid-free paper

12 13 14 15 16 17   10 9 8 7 6 5 4 3 2 1

First Edition

"We let our emotions take over our lives everyday!"

—Colin Cowherd, Nationally Syndicated Radio Host

An Overview

Your *Killer Emotions*

Your emotions can be *killers*! They can kill the accomplishment of your plans, the fulfillment of your dreams, and the attainment of the life that you envision and so dearly want for yourself. Potentially poisonous emotions can also trigger behavior that leads to lower self-esteem and self-worth. Essentially, they can destroy your spirit and your positive energy. Obviously, all of this is extremely bad stuff!

When I was a Harvard undergrad, I saw the very smartest people do some of the most unfathomable, self-destructive, and seemingly "stupid" things.[1] In the process, they destroyed themselves and their chances of enjoying exceedingly bright futures. From this apparent irony, I gleaned the following: Just because a person is intellectually

---

1 For example, some students who seemingly had everything going for them took recreational drugs until they ruined their once razor-sharp minds; committed rebellious acts against their parents, landing the students in jail; or drank to such excess that they became dangerous to themselves and to others.

gifted or wonderfully talented doesn't mean that he or she is in control of his or her emotions. In fact, it can be quite the contrary!

Haven't you, at one time or another, let your *feelings* of hurt, anger, loneliness, resentment, rage, neediness, insecurity, jealousy, and/or hopelessness cloud your best judgment, resulting in your making a disappointing, self-sabotaging, and/or spirit-deflating life choice? If your response is, "Oh yes, unfortunately far too many times," have you considered what led to these life-derailing situations?

The answer may well be that you were energized, catalyzed, and led to act in response to the *energy charges* from potentially poisonous feelings, urges, and impulses because they, at the time, *overpowered* and thereby negated your intellect and your best judgment. You wound up assuaging an intense impulse or urge rather than opting to make a positive life choice. Your actions were not a well thought-out reflection of your very best judgment, as you didn't take into account what you truly want in and for your life. Instead, you made a self-defeating, emotionally charged choice that was in direct contradiction to what you, in more lucid moments, would want to accomplish. And later, upon clearer reflection, you realized once again that you had compromised your life goals and dreams, as well as your physical, psychological, emotional, and/or spiritual well-being! This failure to do what you generally knew was "right" may also have led to a significant diminution of your overall self-esteem, as well as to a substantial decrease in your core confidence to create and enjoy the life that you crave.

Over the past 30 years, I have successfully counseled thousands upon thousands of individuals regarding their most important life and career choices, and there is one thing that almost all of them have in common: They have made crucial, self-defeating or self-sabotaging decisions that they later dearly regretted at a time when their best, clear judgment was clouded by sabotaging emotions, impulses, or urges.

Sometimes we pay little or no price for poor/self-destructive decision-making. However, many times we cause ourselves, our most dearly held goals, and the ones we love severe or irreparable damage because we are unable to think and reason clearly and toxic-emotion-free at pivotal decision-making moments.

Think of *Your Killer Emotions* as your *emotional survival kit*, as it will provide you with a set of clear, tried-and-true *Steps* for acting with absolute intellectual clarity when you are about to make important life and career choices. The key is for you to master your emotions and urges and to turn them into your *allies* when you are making important life choices. One of the ways by which you will accomplish this is by correctly identifying your unique set of very specific *Personal Emotional Triggers*™ (or *PETS*™). As we will discuss, these *PETS* are *so* highly super-charged that they will overpower, and thereby nullify, the less potent, competing, and/or conflicting energy charges of potentially destructive and/or sabotaging emotions, urges, and impulses. As a direct result, you will be free to make crystal-clear life choices and take actions that reflect and effect what you most want for yourself and your life in the long term.

There are some things in life that you can control and some that you can't. I've seen way too many individuals make diminishing, destructive, and/or self-sabotaging life choices because they worried about things that they couldn't control, and they didn't focus—or lost focus—on controlling the things that they could. You absolutely can control your reasoning and evaluative processes, your choices, and your actions—as long as you master the potentially toxic emotions, urges, and impulses that can compromise or totally dismantle your best judgment when you make your life choices.

So, if making truly *great* life choices sounds exciting, beneficial, and/or intriguing, let's get started!

CONTENTS

PART ONE

Your POWER BASE: Some Essential Core
Concepts of Emotion Mastery

When counseling individuals to make *the* very most life-enhancing choices, I have found that it is essential that they have a working knowledge and understanding of the Core Concepts of Emotion Mastery. These Concepts comprise your POWER BASE.

I have always been a huge proponent of building and maintaining a rock-solid foundation of knowledge and understanding *before* undertaking any endeavor—especially if your goal is to successfully navigate the often stormy waters of life. As I want you to be a life-choice-making rock star, let's briefly discuss the Core Concepts before we move on to *The 7 Steps*. Your goal here is to be an active and excited reader, as these Concepts are the underpinnings of *The 7 Steps* that will so very positively change and lift your life!

Here's to developing and shoring up your POWER BASE and your lifelong ability to make gratifying, life-enhancing choices.

Chapter 1

Energy Charges

G enerally, we tend to view emotions from an intellectual standpoint. *Your Killer Emotions*, however, is based upon the *physiology* of emotions, in that it focuses on the often highly potent energy charges triggered by them. For example, whereas we often think of the emotion of "love" in an intellectual sense, we rarely think of it as a catalyzing *physiological force*, and we almost never knowingly and strategically use or channel the exceedingly strong energy charges generated by this emotion to our advantage.

To illustrate what I mean by the physiology of emotions, think about the huge adrenaline rush that you *feel* when something or someone triggers your anger or rage; how sky-high you feel and how supremely motivated you are when you're in love; or how incredibly excited you feel when you secure or attain something you've been dreaming of. You're *charged-up*! For our purposes, what you feel in these instances are the *energy charges* generated by your exceedingly strong emotions.

With the information and *Steps* provided in *Your Killer Emotions*, you can learn how to identify, tap into, harness, and channel the awesome energy charges from your emotions, urges, and impulses, and strategically use them as your allies; as a result, when you are faced with intense, competing energy charges from your potentially toxic emotions, urges, and impulses, you can think clearly and choose to act in a manner that is consistent with the goals that you value the most. Instead of letting your emotion-triggered energies control you, *you can control them*—to your tremendous benefit! You will be able and, in every sense of the word, *empowered*, to attain what you deeply desire, to truly live the life you dream about, and to become the person you ideally want to be.

Mastering potentially sabotaging emotions and their energy charges is your *Emotional Imperative*.

Your *Take-Aways:*

1. The *Steps*, processes, and other information found in this book are based upon the *physiology* of emotions and, therefore, the energy charges triggered by them.

2. You can identify, tap into, harness, and channel the awesome energy charges from your emotions and use them as your allies, enabling and empowering you to think clearly and consistently with your best judgment when you make your life choices.

Chapter 2

The Cognitive Versus the Emotional Components of Making Life Choices

Years ago, I gave a speech about the "Components of Constructive Decision-Making." I discussed the concept of *Framing*™, which we will focus on in great detail later. *Framing* is the formula that I developed in order to enable individuals to control, overpower, and ultimately nullify potentially self-defeating emotions when trying to make their very wisest decisions. At the end of my presentation, one of *Oprah's* producers approached me and basically said, "All of the decision-making theories that I've heard in the past focus on the *intellectual* component of decision-making. But you deal with the *emotions*. And, while most of us intellectually *know* what we should do in a given situation, when strong emotions come into play, we often make terrible decisions. If you can show people how to separate their emotions from their decision-making [processes], you will be able to help a great many people and [thus] make a real contribution!"

Besides offering much-appreciated encouragement, this magnanimous program executive also highlighted two distinctly different influences that can play major roles when you make your life choices:

1. your intellect or what you *know* or *think*; and

2. your emotions, urges, and impulses and/or what you *feel*.

As we shall discuss throughout *Your Killer Emotions*, these two influences can be at absolute odds when you make your life choices. However, as you will see, your *intellect* and *emotions* can work *in concert*, enabling you to attain your most dearly held goals, to live the life that you dream about, and to enjoy the tremendously empowering and energizing feelings of mastering your emotions. This harmonious collaboration is your goal. The key to accomplishing this goal is to diligently practice and effectively perform the skill sets that are presented herein.

Your *Take-Away:*

There are two integral components of making life choices: the intellectual and the emotional.

Chapter 3

Your *Emotional Imperative* and a Brief Discussion of Behaviorism

Let's hearken back to the classic stimulus-response experiment conducted by I. P. Pavlov. As you may remember, Pavlov would introduce a piece of meat to a dog, and the dog would react by salivating. At some point, along with the introduction of the meat, the dog would hear the ringing of a bell. With repetition, the dog began to associate the sound of the bell with the luscious meat. This led to the dog salivating on cue, even when there was no meat in the vicinity. Therefore, Pavlov, through the effective use of positive reinforcement, was able to "condition" a predictable response from the dog. This was very important early work in the field of behaviorism, and we will come back to it later in order to discuss its relevance in connection with mastering your emotions.

Thereafter, B. F. Skinner advanced the field of behaviorism by developing behavioral-conditioning theories for human beings that identify our ability to elicit, to teach, and to learn certain desired human behaviors through the use of positive and negative reinforcement.

Dr. M. Scott Peck enlightened us a good deal further in his brilliant work, *A Road Less Traveled.*[A] Therein, Dr. Peck essentially discussed and celebrated the all-important difference between the automatic reaction elicited from the dog in Pavlov's stimulus-response experiment and a human's ability to not simply react but, instead, to *consciously and knowingly act* when a stimulus is introduced.

Peck discussed the concept of "bracketing," which means that when we are exposed to a stimulus, instead of automatically reacting as Pavlov's pooch did, we as human beings have the ability to take a step back, think, and decide on an appropriate response. According to Dr. Peck and to Dr. Stephen Covey in his landmark book, *7 Habits of Highly Effective Individuals,*[B] it is our gift and ability *to think and choose*—instead of simply automatically reacting in or to a given situation—that makes us human.

I wholeheartedly agree with both Drs. Peck and Covey regarding this point. However, it becomes quite obvious that *thinking, alone, is just not enough* when we want to make our most beneficial life choices, as we are often exposed to certain potentially poison-provoking people, events, thoughts, or situations. In these instances we are often helplessly "all too human," as we let our toxic emotions and urges flood and overtake our intellect, and we wind up making self-sabotaging choices and acting in an ill-considered, damaging way. Therefore, it is *not* enough to just (attempt to) think in these emotion-filled situations when our mental processes are severely weakened or totally dismantled. In these instances, it is essential for you to control and master your emotions and to make them work *for* you so that you can think and evaluate clearly.

So, while *Your Killer Emotions* embraces Dr. Peck's and Dr. Covey's optimistic perspectives regarding our gifts/abilities to think and objectively evaluate people, things, and conditions when we make our choices, as you will glean, *Your Killer Emotions advances* our evolution. It not only acknowledges the cognitive component of making life choices, but it provides you with the essential addition of a set of tried-and-true *Steps,* so that you can make highly beneficial use of your most potent emotion-generated energy charges. As a result, your wisest and best judgment will prevail when you make your all-important life choices.

Your *Take-Away:*

In many instances when you are called upon to make a life choice, you will be flooded with intense, battling, conflicting emotions. Therefore, when making positive choices, you must not only *know* what you want to secure or accomplish with your choices, but you must also be in control of your emotions if you want to make choices that reflect and are consistent with your most highly valued goals.

Chapter 4

How You View Your Emotions, Feelings, Urges, Impulses, and Compulsions

E motions aren't necessarily good or bad per se; they are beneficial if they and their energy charges catalyze and compel you to make a positive and beneficial life choice. Conversely, emotions, impulses, and urges are poisonous and sabotaging if they and their energy charges lead you to make a self-defeating or self-destructive life choice.

As you know, in many instances, the emotion of anger can trigger self-sabotaging behavior from the person who feels angry. For example, there was a very talented individual, "Bill,"[1] whom I have counseled; he had tremendous potential in his chosen field. However, he also had persistent anger-management issues and suffered related setbacks. And, for as many good things as Bill had accomplished at

---

1 Some of the stories, cases, and examples in this book have been fictionalized and altered in order to protect the privacy of the individuals and their families. Please note that the stories, cases, and examples discussed in this book are solely meant to poignantly and memorably illustrate the *Steps*, strategies, and insights presented herein and are not meant to portray any particular person. Persons referenced in this book may be composites or entirely fictitious; thus, references to any real persons, living or dead, are not implied.

his job, ultimately, way too often, when his emotional buttons were pushed, he would "lose his head" and viciously blow up at others. Here's Bill's story:

Bill's employer appreciated his considerable talents and often protected him by downplaying Bill's well-documented work-related blow-ups. But one day, when Bill yet again lost his temper in an exceedingly ugly, vitriolic, and rage-filled manner with a highly regarded employee who threatened to quit if Bill wasn't immediately let go, the employer—in light of the prior, valid complaints of other employees against Bill—had no choice but to terminate Bill's employment. In this instance, in spite of the fact that Bill had exceptional talent and loved his chosen field, it was clear that he couldn't control his temper when certain individuals or situations pushed his emotional buttons. Sadly, within a year, Bill lost another, lesser position with another firm for exactly the same reason: his anger-filled outbursts.

Bill then spent nearly two years applying for less prominent positions, at less desirable firms, with no success. Thereafter, with tremendous bitterness and regret, Bill continued to struggle, as he has had to accept far less rewarding and lucrative positions outside of the field that he loved and was, in many ways, perfectly suited for.

Obviously, this is a clear case in which rage flooded and overpowered someone beyond all reason, thereby obliterating good judgment. At Bill's original firm, he was reprimanded numerous times for his ugly emotional outbursts. Each time, during discussions with the firm's human-resources department, Bill claimed that he "clearly understood" that he couldn't vent his anger against his fellow employees; he *knew* that his outbursts were initially promotion-threatening, and that over time, they had become job-threatening. In one of his final meetings with human resources, Bill had calmly and with great contrition said to the head of that department, as well as to the company's president, that he had thought things through (after his series of anger-related transgressions) and would be "smarter" the next time something or someone upset him. He had then convincingly argued that he truly valued being at such a well-respected firm and was pursuing his dream career there. Over and over again, Bill had said that he *knew* what he needed to do, which was to never again lose his temper or be demeaning or retaliatory toward others.

Because Bill had said all the right things and seemed to really grasp both what he'd done wrong in the past and what he needed to do right in the future, the firm gave him "one last chance" to shape up— an opportunity that he blew just weeks later with his vitriolic blow-up with the well-respected staff employee.

The fact that Bill *knew* what his mistakes were and *knew* how he needed to comport himself in the future made absolutely no difference when the high-voltage energy charges generated by his deep-seated anger triggered his unacceptable and self-sabotaging behavioral pattern. In this case, the emotion of anger and the incredibly powerful charges of energy generated therefrom were indeed poisonous, because they derailed Bill's good intentions and best judgment, and fueled his self-destructive behavior.

On the other hand, years ago, when I was a member of the Eastern Junior Davis Cup tennis team, a teammate of mine, "Chris," was in the midst of losing a crucial match in a totally lackluster manner:

To our team's great dismay, he just didn't seem to care. But then, the most interesting thing happened. His opponent, "Tim," called a couple of Chris's shots out, although they were clearly in. To make matters worse, Tim apparently called the set score incorrectly, giving himself an extra game and taking one away from Chris. So, instead of the score being 4 to 2 in favor of Tim, he called the score as 5 to 1. By this time, Chris and everyone on our team thought that Tim was cheating.

You know the saying, "Let sleeping dogs lie"? Well, Chris became so angry with Tim that it woke Chris up from his apparent malaise and complacency. Chris's anger energized him enough to win the match, 3–6, 6–2, 6–1.

So in Chris's case, anger turned out to be a *beneficial* and *constructive* emotion. The tremendously potent energy charges generated by Chris's anger literally motivated, catalyzed, and fueled him to focus on the match, play his very best tennis, and ultimately defeat someone who triggered his ire.[2]

The lesson here: In these two cases, the potent energy charges generated by the same emotion—anger—triggered two very different forms of *expression*. In Bill's case, it catalyzed and caused him to totally disregard what he knew to be the right choice and behavior for him. Conversely, the anger that Chris felt energized and caused him to act in a totally constructive manner.

So, the insight here is that it's not the emotion in and of itself that is positive or poisonous—it's rather the act that a particular emotion and its energy charges *triggers* that can be beneficial or self-defeating and self-sabotaging. Therefore, it's all in how you are able to *use* the very potent energy charges generated by and from your emotions that will dictate whether you will make a positive life choice or a poisonous one!

Let's now focus on the feeling of love. In many instances, love can inspire and motivate individuals to strive to do wonderfully constructive things, such as being thoughtful of and compassionate toward others, doing charitable work, and being an overall better person— all beautiful expressions of the energy charges generated by this emotion. However, there are also instances when the expression of the emotion of love can be self-sabotaging and self-defeating.

For example, I know a wonderful, kind girl, "Beth," who is blessed to have a tremendous amount of love in her heart and is very open about expressing it. The problem is that on occasion, because Beth

---

2 We later learned that Chris's seemingly indifferent match play was due to a major fight that he had had with his longtime girlfriend a few hours before the match.

is so very in touch with her feelings and so prone to sharing them, she can express her love at inappropriate times. An illustration of this occurred when she met "Kent" on a blind date, which was set up by their mutual friend, "Kiera":

This date was one of Kent's first since emerging from a long-term relationship with someone whom he loved very much. Before the first date, Beth was told very explicitly by Kiera that what Kent wanted and needed was to have a light and breezy dating life until he healed from his fiancée's breaking up with him (because of a lack of physical chemistry.)

The problem here, according to Beth, is that it had been years since she'd found someone like Kent with whom she connected so quickly and deeply. As a result, after her third date with the handsome, funny, and evolved Kent, Beth not only felt incredible love in her heart, but with great ardor, she also expressed it to him. At this point in Kent's life, this was the last thing he wanted to hear and experience. What Kent dearly wanted was air and space; nevertheless, with the best of intentions, what Beth gave him was love-filled smothering. And the more Kent retreated, the more Beth tried to become an integral part of his life—until he felt that it became necessary to have "the talk" with Beth and tell her that he really needed to cool it with her, as he wasn't at all ready for anything serious or structured so soon after his breakup.

I know Kent well, and a year or so later, he confided to me that had he met a "warm, sweet, pretty girl like Beth years earlier," he would have been much more ready to consider being in a serious and committed relationship. He then added, "The timing [of meeting Beth] so soon [after my engagement ended] was terrible!"

In this instance, we see how the energy charges generated from an emotion such as love, which often triggers beneficial life choices and actions, instead triggered a self-defeating life choice and a series of self-destructive acts by Beth.

So, here's the profound problem: Notwithstanding Beth's *clear knowledge* of Kent's recent history and current state of mind (that he was fresh out of a very painful, unwanted breakup of his engagement, and what he wanted and needed at that point in his dating life were air and space), the overwhelming energy charges generated from Beth's need to express her love and/or assuage her feelings of neediness or loneliness totally overpowered her best judgment. The result was that she did the one thing that she would never *knowingly* want to do: drive away someone in whom she was so very romantically interested.

Here's one more story, which I call, "Minding Your Pees and Cues":

"Tommy" was a five-year-old first grader who was playing a competitive game of kickball during his physical-education hour. The score between the teams was tied, and play hour was almost over. Tommy's team was up to bat. His team had runners on first and second base with one out. Tommy was on deck when suddenly, he felt the urge to urinate, as he had the last inning—but this time with much more urgency. The problem was that Tommy didn't want to leave the game, knowing that he would in all likelihood get up to bat and could win the game for his team.

A moment later, with his teammate still at bat, Tommy's conflict became ever more intense: flee and pee, or stay and play, at his peril!

Seconds later, Tommy's need to go to the bathroom became so intense that he could only stand in the on-deck area with his legs tightly crossed. Yet he still chose not to leave the field and forego his turn at bat.

A moment or two later, Tommy's teammate at the plate struck out. So it was Tommy's turn at bat. As the ball was rolled toward Tommy, he uncrossed his thighs and moved to kick the ball. But unfortunately, he could no longer hold it in. He felt a warm stream of liquid run down his leg. What made matters exponentially worse was that Tommy was wearing light-colored slacks, so that the urine stream/stain was evident.

The profound shame that Tommy felt was devastating and self-esteem decimating. In tears, he ran off the field to the bathroom as classmates pointed and laughed. According to Tommy, the absolutely abhorrent visual of him wetting his light-beige slacks in front of his classmates was enough to make him *always* go to the bathroom *first!* from that day on and worry about everything else second.

Tommy's story is another example of how what we perceive as a "negative" emotion—*shame*—can motivate you to make future enhancing life choices and behavioral modifications; and that emotions aren't positive or negative per se. Instead it is the acts that our emotions trigger that determine whether the emotions are beneficial or toxic.

In review, there are four important points to reinforce here:

1. An emotion isn't necessarily positive or negative. It is rather the energy charges generated by that emotion that trigger and fuel either a beneficial or a poisonous *expression* of the emotion—that is, either a beneficial, empowering life choice and act or ones that are self-sabotaging.

2. It is the *expression* of an emotion that can make all the difference as to whether you have a positive, self-esteem-raising result or a self-defeating, self-sabotaging, self-esteem-lowering one.

   An example of this can be seen in the case of Bill, whom we discussed earlier. It was not simply the fact that Bill *felt* anger and/or rage in the workplace that was problematic.

What caused his termination was his uncontrolled and inappropriate *expression* of those feelings in the workplace. So, it is important for you to be continually cognizant of the fact that it is one thing to feel the energy charges generated by a potentially poisonous emotion, but it is quite another to allow those feelings and their particular energy charges to trigger uncontrolled, self-sabotaging actions on your part.

To reiterate, Beth, whom we also just discussed, felt an immediate, extremely strong connection with Kent. Had she kept her intense feelings in check and given Kent his requested and required space, Beth and Kent might still be together today. What sabotaged their relationship was Beth's *uncontrolled* and *self-sabotaging expression* of her feelings/emotions.

As you will later see and experience through the process of *Framing*™, by being conscious and nullifying the power of potentially poisonous emotions and their collective energy charges, you control and keep these emotions in check so that you do not wind up expressing them in a destructive manner.

3. What can be a poisonous expression of an emotion, feeling, or urge in one case might not be one in another situation. The expression's nature depends upon the *context*. Therefore, you must always strive to be aware of and to discern whether it is the appropriate time, place, and/or context to beneficially express a particular emotion, feeling, impulse, or urge. For example, had Beth waited until a more appropriate time to express her strong feelings for Kent, this expression may well have been received in a positive manner instead of in a negative one.

4. You can only be consistently astute and discerning at

choice-making time if you are in control of your emotions, so that you can think, intuit, evaluate, and reason with clarity.

Your *Take-Aways:*

1. It's not the emotion that is positive or poisonous—it's the related choice or course of action that a particular emotion and its energy charges triggers that can be either constructive and life-lifting, or self-defeating and self-sabotaging.

2. Generally, it is the unthinking and/or uncontrolled *expression* of an emotion that can be self-sabotaging.

Chapter 5

How You Treat Emotions, Feelings, Urges, Impulses, Compulsions, and Addictions

As we move forward, let's discuss what we mean by the terms *emotions*, *feelings*, *urges*, *impulses*, *compulsions*, and *addictions*. Emotions can be feelings of love, anger, resentment, jealousy, rage, alienation, betrayal, sadness, hopelessness, neediness, and insecurity. Urges can have a more biological basis, such as the need for sex, food, or physical contact. The impulse or compulsion to smoke, drink alcohol, and engage in recreational drugs, for example, sometimes has both emotional and physical roots, while addiction can be defined as either an actual temporary altering of the brain's chemical balance by virtue of a psychoactive substance (i.e., one that affects the mind) or as a psychological dependency on activities or pursuits such as gambling, work, or even exercise. So, one might ask, "What's the difference among an emotion, an urge, an impulse, and a compulsion?" or "When does a feeling, a need, or an urge repeat itself so often that it becomes a compulsion or an addiction?" Attempting to define and distinguish among feelings, emotions, impulses, urges, and addictions can certainly prove challenging. Let me discuss these ambiguities by way of a story:

A few years ago, I had a discussion with "Brandon." He was about forty-five years old at the time, nice-looking, and articulate. But he felt that he needed to make much better decisions in his romantic encounters. He shared that he had been divorced twice and had suffered through numerous failed relationships. He said that he had taken time to do some deep soul-searching and that he "absolutely knew" why all of his romantic relationships "go to hell," imparting that whenever he became intimate with someone, he eventually had his partners make love to a consistent diet of "soft porn." And once he introduced a pornographic film into the romantic encounter, he needed to have "some hot film playing" as part of his "lovemaking" during every sexual encounter thereafter in order to remain sexually interested and aroused.

What I gathered from Brandon's story was that once he met someone whom he was attracted to, at some point he became flooded with the urge to have sex with the aid of an additional stimulant (the porn). Intellectually, he *knew* that this behavior caused women to leave him time after time. Yet, like clockwork, no matter how much on one level he truly wanted to stay in a relationship with some of these women, when the urge to have sex to porn came to the fore, he was overwhelmed and lost all control and good judgment. Inevitably, each love-interest would eventually depart.

Later, I will discuss how I was able to help Brandon by enabling him to master his emotions/compulsions and their energy charges, but for now, our two questions are:

1. Is Brandon's pattern of self-sabotaging behavior caused by an urge, an emotion, an impulse, a feeling, or a compulsion?; and

2. At what point does the consistent need to satisfy this urge or assuage this impulse or feeling become an addiction?

An in-depth exploration into these questions can require multiple books unto themselves for resolution. However, for us, this study and discussion are academic, as the skill sets that you learn here will empower you to master *all* of your emotions, urges, compulsions, and feelings—and their potent energy charges—regardless of what labels we decide to use. Additionally, you will be able to rely on your very wisest, well thought-out judgment when you make your life choices, whether or not we call a string of the same or similar past self-sabotaging choices and acts a pattern, a script, or an addiction.

As we move forward, we will use the term "energy charges" to refer to the energy generated by your emotions, feelings, urges, impulses, and compulsions. Additionally, in many instances, we will simply use the term "emotions" as our shorthand for emotions, feelings, urges, impulses, and compulsions.

Your *Take-Aways:*

1. For our purposes, we will view and treat the terms "emotions," "feelings," "urges," "impulses," and "compulsions" in the same way. *Your Killer Emotions* will show you how you can master all of them.

2. We will use the term "energy charges" in order to refer to the energy charges generated by your emotions, feelings, urges, impulses, and compulsions.

3. On many occasions, we will simply use the term "emotions" in order to denote emotions, feelings, impulses, urges, and compulsions.

Chapter 6

Your Killer Emotions Timeline

Your Killer Emotions Timeline is comprised of three very specific phases:

Phase One is devoted to teaching *The Prevent Offense*, which is comprised of four tried-and-true *preparatory Steps* that you will take months, weeks, and/or days *before* you are called upon to make a life choice. These *Steps* are specifically designed to *prevent* you and your intellect from being flooded and/or derailed by high-voltage, poisonous energy charges when you make key life choices sometime in the future.

Phase Two presents and discusses the two *Steps* that you will take in order to master your poisonous emotional-energy charges at *Crunch Time!*, which is that point in time when you are faced with making a life choice.

Phase Three provides the *Step* for you to take *after* you have made a life choice. It is a means for you to rework, hone, and/or polish your emotion-mastery and life-choice-making skills.

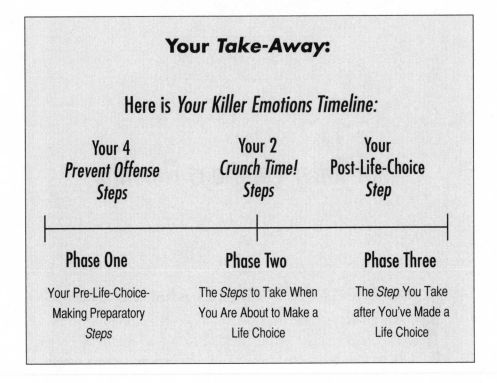

Your *Take-Away:*

Here is *Your Killer Emotions Timeline:*

Your 4 *Prevent Offense Steps*	Your 2 *Crunch Time!* *Steps*	Your *Post-Life-Choice Step*
Phase One	**Phase Two**	**Phase Three**
Your Pre-Life-Choice-Making Preparatory *Steps*	The *Steps* to Take When You Are About to Make a Life Choice	The *Step* You Take after You've Made a Life Choice

Chapter 7

The Importance of Being *Ready* to Grow

B y virtue of my 30 years of counseling experience, I've learned that individuals must be psychologically, emotionally, and intellectually *ready* to grow. As many who have mastered their emotions have later in essence told me: Because they were in the "right" place to take intellectual and emotional ownership of or responsibility for their lives, it was exponentially easier for them to be clear about what they wanted and disciplined enough to make it happen.

I assume that you are reading this book for a reason: because you're *ready* to take charge of your life choices—both on an intellectual and an emotional level—and to materially enhance and lift the quality of your life!

So let's do it! and move on to *The 7 Steps of Emotion Mastery*.

PART TWO

The 7 Steps of Emotion Mastery

The 7 Steps of Emotion Mastery

Your 4 Pre-*Crunch Time! Steps*

The Prevent Offense

Step 1. Identify Your Most Potent *Personal Emotional Triggers* (*Your PETS*)

Step 2. Be Anticipatory: Effectively Anticipate That You Will Have to Make Certain Future, *Conscious* Life Choices

Step 3. Construct Your Future *Frisuals*™—The Vehicle(s) That Will Enable You to Consistently Make Life-Enhancing Choices

Step 4. Adjust the Voltage of the Energy Charges That You Will Channel into Your *Frisuals*

Your 2 *Crunch Time!* Steps

Step 5. When Possible, Review Your *Crunch Time! Reminder List*

Step 6. Make a *Golden/Truthful* Life Choice

Your Post-*Crunch Time!* Step

Step 7. Review Your Life-Choice Process

Your 4 *Prevent Offense Steps*:
The *Steps* That Prepare You to Make Future *Golden* and *Truthful* Life Choices

The Prevent Offense

I n pro football, when a team is winning and wants to protect its lead late in the game, it often employs a strategy called a "prevent defense." Essentially, this is a defense designed to at worst give up mid-sized gains by the opponent, but not a "big play" that can change the outcome of the game. In your quest to master your emotions, you will want to take advantage of a strategy I call *The Prevent Offense*, which is designed to enable you to prevent major derailments when you make future life choices.

The Prevent Offense is a set of *preparatory Steps* that you take days, weeks, and/or months in advance of your having to make a life choice, or a series of life choices. By engaging in this proactive strategy, you are taking a clear, well thought-out offensive stance in order to *prevent* potentially sabotaging emotion-generated energy charges from clouding or overtaking your intellect and your ability to reason logically and constructively at some future *Crunch Time!*.

The following 4 *Steps* comprise your *Prevent Offense*.

STEP 1

Identify Your Most Potent
Personal Emotional Triggers™ (Your PETS™)

Your Gold and *Your Truth*: Their Extraordinary Energy-Charge Potency

Throughout *Your Killer Emotions*, we use the terms *Your Gold* and *Your Truth*. *Your Gold* shall encompass your most highly valued goals and dreams. It is what motivates you the very most. *Your Truth* is your vision of both the life that you most deeply want for yourself and the person who you most truly want to be. It is a vision that truly inspires and motivates you.

Whereas *Your Gold* is most easily understood as the tangible things, positions, or goals that you most want to attain, *Your Truth* is an idealized, or best self. Additionally, always keep in mind that this is *Your* Gold and *Your* Truth, and no one else's. These aspirations are unique to you! They are not what others—a parent, spouse, significant other, or close friend—want for you and/or impose upon you. They are what truly motivate *you*!

You will see as you progress that it is absolutely essential, when you go through *The 7 Steps of Emotion Mastery*, to identify and work with the things, people, events, and goals that you want the very most, love the very most, fear the very most, abhor the very most, shame you the very most. These trigger your very strongest emotion-generated energy charges, which you will then use/channel in order to enable you to overpower and negate the energy charges from the potentially poisonous emotions that can cloud/dismantle your best intellectual judgment.

So by identifying what truly motivates, moves, and excites you— your purest *Gold* and *Truth*—you will be able to tap into and harness your very purest, strongest energy charges. And as you will soon see, the stronger the energy charges that you can harness and tap into, the greater the chances that you will be able to nullify the potency and efficacy of the energy charges generated by your potentially poisonous/sabotaging emotions.

As you move forward, here is what you want to absorb and remember:

1. *Your Gold* and *Your Truth* are the things, people, goals, thoughts, and occurrences that motivate you the very most. As a result, they contain your very strongest emotion-generated energy charges;

2. The more potent *Your Gold* and *Your Truth*, the more potent the energy charges with which you can work—it is therefore essential to *always* identify them in their purest form;

3. The more potent the energy charges that you can tap into and channel (which we will soon discuss), the easier it will be for you to overpower and nullify the ones generated from your potentially poisonous emotions that have led or can lead you to make self-defeating or self-sabotaging life choices;

4. As a result, you will be free and empowered to make intellectually crystal-clear life choices that reflect *Your Gold, Your Truth*, and your very best, well-reasoned judgment.

Your *Take-Aways:*

1. *Your Gold* is comprised of your most highly valued goals and dreams. *Your Truth* is your very personal vision of the life that you most deeply want and the person who you truly want to be.

2. Your most motivating *Gold* and *Truth* generate your highest-voltage energy charges, which you will want to tap into and harness when you desire to overpower and thereby nullify the energy charges generated by your potentially poisonous emotions.

3. *Golden* and *Truthful* choices and acts reflect and embody *Your Gold* and *Your Truth*, respectively.

Your PETS (Your Personal Emotional Triggers)

Your Gold + Your Truth = Your PETS. Therefore, *Your PETS* are those certain unique people, events, things, experiences, information, and aspirations that trigger the strongest emotion-generated energy reactions within you. *Your PETS* touch and strike your deepest and most profound emotional, psychological, and intellectual chords. They are what you value and what motivate you *the* very most!

O.K. Let's now use some real-life examples of how harnessing and tapping into the tremendous energy charges of *Your PETS* can be a transformational, behavioral game-changer.

Below are three personal stories. In connection with Story 1, please keep in mind that one of my most powerful *Personal Emotional Triggers* is that I ABSOLUTELY *HATE!* the thought of being in a hospital as a patient, waiting to be operated on for a life-threatening illness or injury. This hypothetical situation is one of my biggest *fears.* And staying healthy and out of hospitals (as a patient) is one of my most cherished *PETS* (or values).

STORY 1.

Years ago, my car had an analogue cell phone, which I placed against my ear for hours a day as I spoke with clients. After many months of prolonged use of this phone, I began to get strong headaches after phone calls. Maybe it was just a coincidence, but I was certain that I could feel some force (radiation) coming through the receiver on that phone, as my ear felt "funny" each time.

One day, an acquaintance, who happened to be an executive at a major cell-phone company that we all know, off-handedly mentioned the tremendous amount of insurance that his company had taken out in anticipation of the huge number of people who will possibly contract brain cancer as a result of holding their phones up to their ears for extended periods of time.

To say that this individual's remark *rocked* my world would be a vast understatement. So the next day, I went to see my doctor about my headaches. After examining me, he said, "Everything looks O.K., but I'm going to send you to get a brain scan, just to be safe."

I cannot adequately articulate what the thought and all-too-vivid visual of my undergoing brain surgery did to me, but needless to say, it scared the living breath out of me!

A couple of days later, I went to the imaging center for my examination. During the brain-scan procedure, I established a good rapport with the primary technician. After the completion of the procedure, sensing that he could put my fears to rest, the technician came to me and said, "I just want to let you know, you're O.K.! But trust me, those cell phones can kill you—especially those analogues!"

Incredibly relieved and thankful, but still shaken from having exposed myself to what seemed to be a very significant danger, I made a resolution: From that day on, I would *never again!* put my cell phone up against my ear. I would instead either use a headset or I would put the phone on speaker mode—so as to have as much separation from the radiation as possible.

What we can glean from this story is the following:

1. My *PETS* or my *Personal Emotional Triggers* in this case were:

   a. my powerful fear of being a patient in a hospital, treated for a LIFE-THREATENING CONDITION!;[3]

   b. my powerful fear of having BRAIN CANCER!;

   c. my powerful fear of having to go through BRAIN SURGERY!;

   d. my NOT WANTING TO DIE!; and

   e. my fervent desire to LIVE A LONG, HEALTHY LIFE!

2. These incredibly strong, highly emotionally charged *PETS* struck the deepest chord within me;

3. This experience compelled me to break my behavioral pattern or script of always holding my cell phone to my ear during my phone conversations; and

4. This experience and these particular *PETS* from that day forward motivated me to make the life choice to no longer subject myself to the potentially cancer-causing radiation of (analogue) cell phones. As a result, a beneficial behavioral modification took place.

---

3 Throughout this book, I identify individuals' *PETS* in capital letters. I ask my clients when they make their *Lists* to CAPITALIZE the people, things, goals, and events that motivate them the very most. I have found that this form of identification and highlighting may well increase a person's motivation and often results in having these *PETS* stay in one's consciousness in a most memorable and impactful way.

STORY 2.

Throughout my mom's life, she was late for everything: school; work; appointments; her sister's wedding; even her own wedding. This was her behavioral script and status quo until one day, about seven years into my parents' marriage. On that night, my mom was unconscionably late for her date with my dad. Their plan on that snowy, blustery, cold evening was to have dinner and see a Broadway play. However, as a result of my mom's extreme tardiness, my dad wound up standing out-side the restaurant for over two hours, waiting for and worrying about my mom. When she finally arrived, too late for dinner, my dad was frozen and nearly apoplectic. As they entered the theatre, they were told that they had already missed the first twenty minutes of the play. My dad wisely held in his anger and said nothing to my mom for the remainder of the evening.

The next day, my dad, in a much calmer state, came into my mom's dressing room as she was applying her make-up. "Betty," he began, "I don't know what to say . . . . Your behavior is an absolute mystery to me. If you were stupid, then I could understand, and I might forgive you. But you're one of the most intelligent people I know. And gener-ally, I think you're a really nice person. So I ask you: How can you be so downright *mean*? To *me*? How could you let me wait on a street corner on such a freezing-cold night? It's beyond me. I can't begin to tell you how hurt I am. I wouldn't do to an enemy what you did to me. How can you be so uncaring, so impossibly *mean*? How could you? . . ."

My dad then turned and left the room. My mom was stunned. She had never before thought of herself as inconsiderate or *mean*. For my mom, *mean* was the key word and trigger—her *PET*. Being called *mean* bothered her tremendously. For some time afterwards, my mom wondered why she was so disturbed when my dad said that she was *mean*. Then it hit her like a ton of bricks. She associated the word with her mother, whom she abhorred! Her mother had hated her since the day she was born. Her mother had physically and emotionally abused her throughout her childhood. My mom perceived her mother as the "Queen of Mean," and that's why the word struck a primal chord deep down in her psyche. In no way would my mom *ever* want to be like her mother! That was it. That's why she was *so* upset at having been called *mean*. Then my mom had another breakthrough: She had tried to emulate her loving dad in every way possible, and her dad was ALWAYS LATE!

Appearing to be mean, with all of its horribly negative associations and connotations, was the *PET* that shattered my mom's toxic behavioral scripting. She *never* wanted to be like the mother she detested. So on that day, she made the life choice to never be late again. And from that day on, in almost every instance, not only has my mom not been late for her engagements, but she has arrived early!

She says that she has accomplished this extremely positive behavioral change by thinking about being (perceived as) mean each time that she has an appointment. The super high-voltage energy charges of the *PET* of being thought of as *mean*, motivate and catalyze her to begin to get ready for her engagements in a timely fashion, so that she will always be on time.

To review: My mom's newfound ability to clearly see and act consistently with her *Gold* (to not be perceived as mean) and her *Truth* (to be a kind and thoughtful person) became a reality after my dad triggered a huge emotional reaction in my mom, compelling her to break her highly toxic pattern of behavior. The key here is that my dad's words to my mom were so *highly emotionally charged* that they overpowered the compulsion that led her to always be late.

Please note that four processes took place here:

1. My mom identified/recognized that her *PET* was that she *abhorred* being called and perceived as *mean*;

2. She used this highly super-charged *PET* to *motivate*

herself to (strive to) never be late again. For my mom, the *PET* of *not being mean*!—as she perceived her mother to be—acted like highly potent dynamite in blowing up a figurative railroad track of deeply embedded, destructive scripting;

3. As a result, my mom's self-sabotaging behavioral pattern in this area was broken and conquered, and the beneficial life choice to consistently arrive on time and not keep people waiting (interminably) was the beautiful result; and

4. A highly beneficial piece of behavior modification took place.

STORY 3.

"Karissa" was a corporate executive who had custody of three young children from her first marriage. Two years after her divorce from her first husband, she married "Daryl," who had custody of his four children.

Apparently, right from the start, there was tremendous marital discord, and Daryl reacted by becoming an absentee dad to all seven children. This left Karissa as the primary breadwinner and essentially as a single parent. The stress that Karissa experienced was tremendous. The five-foot seven-inch Karissa, who weighed one hundred and thirty pounds when she married Daryl, ballooned to two hundred and twenty. The added weight caused all sorts of additional problems for her, both as an employee in the workplace and as a parent who wanted and needed to run and play with her young children.

For over a year, Karissa thought about and tried to lose weight with no tangible success. Then one day, her seven-year-old biological son, "Bradley," approached her with tears in his eyes. Karissa immediately sat him down and asked him what was wrong. Bradley, with tears now streaming down his cheeks, answered, "Mommy, I don't want you to die!

Please don't die!" Karissa, shocked by the trauma Bradley was experiencing and by what he was saying, said, "Bradley, sweetie, why would you think that I'm going to die?" Bradley responded, "Because you're *so* heavy, Mommy! I'm afraid you'll have a heart attack and die, and with Dad not around, I have *no one* but you! I'm scared, Mommy! *Please* don't leave me, Mommy! *Please!*"

According to Karissa, Bradley's fears so upset and jarred her that over the next two years, she lost more than eighty pounds. Once again, this is an example of how the right *PET* can generate such high-voltage energy charges within you that it will break up your toxic emotional, psychological, and/or intellectual scripting and status quo, as well as fuel your *Golden* and *Truthful* life choices.

But there is another tremendously important insight here: In the last two stories, my dad (intuitively) and Bradley (unknowingly) were able to identify the right motivating and high-voltage *PETS* that, in every way, emotionally moved my mom and Karissa, respectively. These *PETS* broke their self-sabotaging behavioral patterns, enabling and empowering them to thereafter make constructive life choices. The key here is for *you* to correctly identify and tap into the huge, emotion-generated energy charges of *Your PETS*, so that *you* can overpower and nullify the potentially destructive and/or self-sabotaging energy charges that have perpetually led you back to your toxic behavioral scripts at *Crunch Time!*. Once you can break this *scripting*, you are then free to think clearly and make *Golden* and *Truthful,* value-based life choices.

Your *Take-Aways:*

1. *Your Gold* and *Your Truth* comprise *Your PETS.*

2. *Your PETS* are those people, events, dreams, goals, outcomes, and information that strike such a deep chord in your psyche—triggering extremely strong, emotion-generated energy charges—that they motivate and catalyze you to act.

3. *Your PETS* have the awesome power to break up your poisonous behavioral patterns, so that you are then free to consciously make life choices that are consistent with *Your Gold* and *Your Truth*.

Know *Your Truth* and *Gold*—Stone Cold!

I have often heard people express the following concept:

> "In life, it is just as important to know what you truly don't want, as it is to know what you dearly do."

As you will glean, what you want and what you don't—what you cherish and what you loathe—comprise *Your Gold* and *Truth*, which will generate highly potent energy charges of which you can make great beneficial use. Both sides of the equation will have tremendous value to you as you begin to master your emotions.

Your next foundation-building block is to understand that if your goal is to make life choices that reflect and bring about what you truly want in your life, and to evolve into the person you truly want to be, you must take all of the focused time necessary to identify:

1. what you *most dearly* want and value;

2. what you absolutely *do not* want in and for your life; and

3. what you need in order to be truly happy and at peace.

Finding the answers to these profound questions is crucial for at least two compelling reasons:

1. If you *know* what you truly want and need in your life (the cognitive requirement for making *Golden* and *Truthful* life choices), you can then make choices that are consistent with these wants and needs. Essentially, it's always easier to attain something when you can visualize the endgame; and

2. When faced with making a life choice, there will be many times when you and your intellect will be flooded by the energy charges of conflicting and potentially poisonous emotions. As you will soon see, the positive catalyzing energy charges generated by the people, things, and events that you hold most dear; as well as the negative energy charges generated by the people, things, and events that you most fear or abhor, can enable and empower you to override the emotion-generated energy charges that would other-wise trigger you to make self-defeating and self-sabotaging life choices (the emotional component of making *Golden* and *Truthful* life choices). Or put another way, if you can identify the things, people, thoughts, and/or events that motivate you the very most, these motivational energies will lead you to make life choices that are consistent with these motivations.

I'm sure that at one time or another in your life, you have iden-tified something that you dearly wanted, such as a new or first car, a vacation, a cool piece of clothing, or a new home, and, by mak-ing wise choices regarding the allocation of your limited resources, you saved up enough money to purchase it. In these instances, your vision of obtaining the thing you *most* wanted generated the highly

motivating energy charges that fueled and thereby empowered you to
be disciplined and clear-thinking about your monetary choices.

But what about the things that you most disdain, fear, or loathe?
As we have already shown and as you will continue to see, these, too,
are *Your Gold*. They will also produce catalyzing motivating energy
charges that will compel and inevitably lead you to make *Golden/
Truthful* choices. For example, years ago I heard an interview with
a legendary athlete, in which he was asked: "What has led you to
win as consistently and for as long as you have?" To my surprise
and to the best of my recollection, this revered athlete essentially
responded, "Fear. When I go onto the court, I'm afraid I'll lose, so
I'm driven to win."

For one of the most successful athletes ever, the all-powerful emotion of fear[4]—being afraid to lose and abhorring the feeling of losing—produced exceedingly strong, motivating energy charges. These
charges fueled him to accomplish extraordinary things with his talents and to reach tremendous heights in his chosen profession.

Just as my mom materially altered her behavior of always being
late because she couldn't stand the thought of and feared being like
her mom, this athlete was able to use the *PET* of fear as his ally by
tapping into, harnessing, and channeling the awesome energy charges
generated within him by this emotion. Similarly, you too can tap into
the tremendous motivating energy charges generated from things,
people, and/or events that you can't stand or that you fear, disdain,
and abhor in order to supply you with the requisite overpowering,

---

4 The emotion of fear can be one of your greatest impediments to moving forward with your
life and growing; however, as we will soon discuss, when the oftentimes high-voltage energy
charges generated by fear are channeled into your choice-making processes, they can be
one of the most potent motivating forces to empower you to achieve great things. That's one
paradox of fear. Another paradoxical quality of fear is that it can catalyze you to lift your life
in the most positive way; and yet, as we will discuss, it is also one of the "lowest" forms of
motivational energy.

emotion-generated energy charges that will enable you to consistently make positive choices.

> **"The key to identifying your *Gold* and *Truth*,**
> **lies in you being an effective sleuth!"**

Let's now go on to your quest to mine your purest, and therefore your most energy-rich, *Gold* and *Truth*. So, how do you go about accomplishing this? First, by taking the focused, quiet time necessary to dig down, heart-and-soul deep, in order to truly mine and identify the people, things, and events that will make your heart sing!, as well as the people, things, and events that you most fear, are repulsed by, are ashamed of, and the like. Unquestionably, pondering these questions takes time and requires you to be disciplined. But always remember that if you can mine your purest *Gold* and *Truth* (*Your PETS*), you have taken a major step toward attaining the life you dream about and becoming the person you truly want to be. Both are incredible payoffs for the time you will invest in being an astute, patient, effective *Gold* and *Truth* miner. So know that your time cannot be better spent!

During your mining explorations, you can ask yourself some of the following questions:

1. What do I deeply want in my life?

2. Who do I specifically want in my life?

3. What kinds of people do I not want in my life?

4. What do I most want to accomplish in the short term?

5. What do I most want to accomplish in the long run?

6. Ideally, what kind of person would I like to be?

7. Ideally, what would I do in and with my life?

8. What do I want to change about myself or improve upon?

9. What do I love about myself and want to safeguard?

10. What do I cherish above all else?

11. What do I fear above all else?

12. What do I loathe/abhor above all else?

13. What or whom do I absolutely not want in my life?

14. What am I ashamed of?

15. What do I hate about myself and want to eliminate?

16. What are the gifts, talents, and accomplishments of others that I would like to emulate?

17. If I could have three wishes in my life, what would they be?

18. What truly moves me? If I had "do-overs," what actions of mine would I revisit?

19. What did I do wrong, such that I want to replay these life choices?

20. What brings me the greatest, deepest happiness?

21. What makes me the angriest?

22. What makes me the saddest?

23. What brings me, or would bring me, the deepest lasting peace and contentment?

24. What would my ideal life be like?

After you have carefully considered these questions, as practice, try making two *Lists*:

- The first *List* should include the top five things that you most dearly want in and for your life. Write down *what will make your heart sing*!

- The second *List* should contain five of the things that you absolutely detest and abhor, and that you absolutely *do not* want for yourself or in your life.

These can be your initial *PET Lists*.[5]

O.K. Time to make your *Lists*. Doing so comprehensively is highly recommended for at least three reasons:

1. *List*-making helps you to be a more reflective, active, and effective participant in this oh-so-important process;

2. When you write something down or type it, you can see and absorb it. As a result, the *Gold* that you have mined may very well be much more memorable for you; additionally, you will likely feel as though you've accomplished a real, tangible, enabling first step in your quest to attain *Your Gold* and live *Your Truth*; and

3. You can review and, when appropriate, amend your *Lists* in the future so that they accurately reflect your then current, most potent *Gold* and *Truth*.

O.K.! Time to construct your *Lists* and be the most effective *Gold* and *Truth* miner possible in order to identify what individuals, events, thoughts, and things will compel you to make highly beneficial life choices!

When you have carefully completed some or all of your *Lists*, check

---

5 You can download these *PET Lists* by visiting the Web site for *Your Killer Emotions* (www. yourkilleremotions.com).

them for purity, because with purity comes potency. One way to do a "purity check" is to ask yourself whether you have been totally honest in your mining and *List* compilation. If you have not been stone-cold real for any reason, the potency of your *Gold* will be diluted—as will its power charge—and everything that you do thereafter will be compromised or negatively affected as well. So purity is paramount!

To this end, here are some questions whose answers require you to dig down deep. Non-defensively, and with great courage and pure passion for living your ideal life, ask yourself:

1. Do my *Lists* truly reflect who I am and what I most deeply want?;

2. Is there any reason why (e.g., fear of failure or fear of success) I have not identified my purest *Gold*?; and

3. Have I compromised my responses in any way because I'm being influenced by what others want from or expect of me?

If after careful and honest review of your *Lists* you need to amend some of your responses or change the order of some responses so as to make sure that *the* most motivating energy-charged responses are at the top of your *List*, please take the time necessary to do so.

Your next step is to visualize, as clearly as possible, the realization of all of your *Golden/Truthful* responses. For example, below are some of the pieces of *Gold* that individuals whom I have counseled have identified:

1. winning a gold medal at the Olympics;

2. fitting into that sexy bikini/swimsuit that I saw while shopping last week;

3. my daughter/son being abducted in the park because I wasn't paying attention to her/him;

4. being and acting exactly the opposite of my dad, whom I loathe;

5. being diagnosed with throat/lung cancer caused by years of smoking, thereby seriously jeopardizing my ability to be with my children/grandchildren as they grow up;

6. my mother/father passing away before I've taken the time to:

   a. reconcile with her/him;

   b. spend any quality time with her/him; and

   c. tell her/him how much I love her/him;

7. being blessed with a loving, close-knit family;

8. evolving into someone who is a bright light in others' lives and a person committed to being of service to others;

9. creating and owning one of the most popular restaurants in the city, thereby fulfilling my dream;

10. being clear, clean, and sober;

11. finally getting over the anger, rage, and bitterness that festered within me, and learning to forgive;

12. losing weight and growing to feel good—or even great—about how I look!;

13. making conscious choices to surround myself with those who lift me spiritually, psychologically, and/or emotionally, and to let go of those who consistently let me down, diminish me, demean me, limit me, and are toxic;

14. being able to afford to buy the home of my dreams;

15. no longer feeling compelled to smoke.

As you make your *Lists*, continue to picture and feel the attainment of *Your Gold* and *Your Truth* . . . over and over again. Let your smile be wide and the song in your heart and soul be sweet as you visualize yourself triumphantly making *Golden* and *Truthful* life choices!

Additionally, over time, as you mine, reevaluate, add to, and revise your *Gold* and *Truth* (*Your PET*) *Lists*, it is essential to keep the most motivating *PETS* at the top of each one. Your revisions reflect important changes over time in your value system or new truths you've discovered by digging down even deeper and becoming an even more talented and astute *PET* identifier and evaluator.

These are all beneficial and necessary steps in order for you to trigger and tap into *the* most powerful emotion-generated energy charges at decision-making or *Crunch Time!* so that you inevitably, and with great consistency, make *Golden* and *Truthful* life choices.

Your *Take-Aways:*

1. Take the necessary time to mine *Your Gold* and *Truth* and make the appropriate *PET Lists* with your most highly valued *Gold* and *Truth* at the top.

2. These steps are necessary in order to identify *your most potent PETS*, as the energy charges from these *PETS* are the ones that will motivate you *the most* to make a certain desired and beneficial choice.

PET Identification

To illustrate the *Gold/Truth*-mining process, here is a story about my dear friend "Danielle" and her need to mine and re-mine her *Gold* and *Truth* in order to make the most constructive and beneficial life choices for her and her son, "Patrick":

Danielle is a forty-seven-year-old single mom with a fifteen-year-old son, Patrick. During early 2009, Danielle and her husband, "Ed," separated, due in large part to Ed's destructive and highly unsavory behavior. Because of his alleged highly disturbed and disturbing acts, Ed had been out of work for over five years, severely draining the couple's savings. During this time, the family for the most part lived on Danielle's income as a real-estate broker.

Danielle is an extremely bright, savvy, attractive individual who has always been driven and has excelled professionally. Upon her separation from Ed, Danielle ramped up her real-estate business, and for the first year-and-a-half, selling homes was relatively lucrative for her. But when the 2008 recession hit and sales came to a near standstill, Danielle's father implored her to "get out of real estate and find a job in a stable company that can give you and Patrick the guaranteed income and job security you need!"

Sometime thereafter, I visited with Danielle, who said, "Ken, I'm *panicked and scared to death*! I've lost nearly half of my 401K savings, and I'm not selling any homes. My dad's all over me to bag the real-estate business. I'm totally responsible for my son's support. If I don't pay for his schooling, no one will. My dad wants me to take a boring corporate job. For the first time in my life, I'm really scared! Terrified! I feel like I'm being forced to make a snap decision, and I can't think straight. My dad's called a couple of his corporate buddies and asked them as a favor to please find a position for me. I have interviews with them next week. But I know I'll *hate* the jobs! I've worked so hard to build up my real-estate business. I *hate* to leave it all behind. You're the decision-making guru. What do I do?"

I responded to Danielle in the following way: "O.K. Let's relax and think this out clearly and carefully. Often, when you're overcome by fear or panic and have to make a decision, one of two things happens:

1. You're *frozen* by your fear, so you can't or don't think or act rationally;[6] or

2. You react without thinking clearly and take an inappropriate, or worse, a self-sabotaging action.

But you aren't going to do either!

O.K. Let me ask you some questions, and you will figure this out. First of all, I'm gathering that what you want is to continue to earn your living by running your real-estate business and helping your clients buy and sell homes. (Her *PET.*) Is this correct?"

"Absolutely, yes! That's what I want!"

"O.K., you have now identified what I call your second purest piece of *Gold*. Obviously, your purest *Gold* is your being able to adequately support your son and yourself."

Danielle then responded that if she didn't have the awesome, sole responsibility of making sure that her son was taken care of, she would take a risk and stay in real estate; but she believed that she couldn't take that chance under the circumstances.

I then asked her, "So, in your sound, reasonable judgment, is there any way you see yourself doing enough real-estate business in the foreseeable future to support you and your son?"

"No, I don't," she responded, sadly.

"O.K. Just your knowing that valuable information is your *Gold*! Let's keep going, Danielle. Tell me more about where your professional passions lie."

"Well, I love real estate. But, you know, I grew up in the television-production business, because of my grandfather. I loved that, too! But,

---

6 The concept of "frozen by fear" is discussed in detail starting on pages 120-124 and continuing on pages 187-189.

when I had Patrick, I had to be home much more, so I left TV production. That was about fifteen years ago. It's been a while."

"O.K.! You now have unearthed another piece of *Gold*. You loved being in the television-production industry. Great! What facet of it excited you?"

"Sales. Selling shows to local station managers around the country. I loved being involved with the individuals who created the shows, as well as with the producers who gave the shows life. I really loved going around the country, meeting with and explaining to the local station managers why they should buy our show! I'd always come up with novel sales approaches. Even more than the shows, I just loved being with smart, interesting people."

As Danielle answered this last question, you could see her light up with enthusiasm and animation.

I continued, "Great! Now tell me why you love the real-estate business so much."

"I love working with people. I love looking at and marketing homes. I get a real thrill when I put people in homes they love! I'm a born marketer! And, once again, I just love being with people!"

"O.K., Danielle, we have now identified three more pieces of your *Gold*:

1. You, first and foremost, love working with and being around *people*;

2. You love and have a great talent in *marketing*; and

3. It appears that you won't be happy or thrive in a structured office job not centered around dealing with people."

Danielle enthusiastically responded, "You got it!" Her demeanor continued to brighten as she saw the progress we were making and all of the positives that were indentified during our discussions.

I continued, "Any other *Gold* you can think of?"

"I want to do something that I love and can stay in for a long time. I feel that way about real estate. I'm great when I'm passionate about something. Then I'm engaged and I'll work like crazy! With no man in my life, I really want to love what I do professionally. You know, real estate got me out meeting all sorts of wonderful people. I love that!"

"O.K.," I continued, "what *don't* you want?"

"A job I don't care about in a field I have no interest in. But my dad is telling me I *must* make a move now, even if I work for a bank! Oh my God, I *hate* the thought!"

"All right! It's time to make your *Gold List*. Here are your priorities, as I see them:

1. to be a loving and responsible mother to Patrick and adequately support you both;

2. to do something you're passionate about;

3. to not be one of those individuals who settles because they're too lazy or afraid to seek out and secure what they truly want;

3. to work with interesting people and use your great marketing skills;

4. to have a career that allows you to spend enough time with Patrick;

5. to keep your real-estate business, if possible;

6. if your real-estate business isn't viable at this point, to return to the television-production industry; and

7. to have a career with longevity.

How's our *List*?"

"I love it! Right on target!"

"O.K., let's explore three parallel paths or *Choreographies* (sets of highly strategic, calculated *Steps*), as time for you is of the essence. Since staying in real estate is your purest and most potent career *Gold*: Is there any avenue that you haven't yet explored that can keep you afloat in your chosen field? I know the economy's terrible, but certain new conditions often create new needs and niches. Is there any new need out there that you can fill?"

Danielle thoughtfully responded, "Well, there *is* a great opportunity for the people with expendable income to buy homes as investments at rock-bottom prices! It's far safer for them than putting their money in today's stock market!"

"It sounds right to me. How much money do you have saved up?"

"About enough to support us for a year."

"Good. Our first exploration track is for you to figure out the feasibility of refocusing your real-estate business on bringing attractive investment properties to individuals with expendable income. You've always dealt with an upscale clientele; hopefully, they're into having you find some sound investments for them. Do your homework, and see if you can make a go of it."

"I *love* that idea!"

"At the same time, let's you and I call all of our contacts in the television-production arena. Hopefully there's a position at one of these companies that can take advantage of your gifts and will make your heart sing! And, if there is, you can put your real-estate business on hold until conditions are better. But who knows, maybe you'll have a long-term career in production?!"

"I'm so excited, Ken. I feel so much better already! A little hope is a great thing! Seriously, thank you!"

"Danielle, you're always welcome!"

"What do I do about going to the meetings my dad has set-up for me?"

"That's your third exploration path. Go to them. You have only two. See what happens. You never know! But put the great majority of your time, energy, and brilliance into seeing if you can create a new real-estate niche for yourself, and spend the rest of your time getting meetings and interviewing with production companies."

"I'm ecstatic, Ken. We now have a crystal-clear game plan or *Choreography*, as you call it. A vision!"

"Remember the song we heard years ago, 'I can see clearly now, the rain is gone'? Well, with clarity comes calm. No more panic!"

"I can see and think clearly now! Yay!"

"O.K., time to get started doing your real-estate research and setting up production-company interviews. Give it all you've got!"

"You've got it, chief! I'll call you with my progress!"

"Sounds great!"

Fortunately for Danielle, within four weeks, three positive developments took place:

1. Her research and best judgment told her that being involved with any form of real-estate business at such a precarious financial time would be too risky given the circumstances and her obligations (As we have discussed, learning what you *don't* want or *shouldn't* do is also pure *Gold*.);

2. Danielle interviewed for and was offered a newly created position in affiliate sales for a major production company. With tremendous excitement, passion, and gratitude, she accepted the offer; and, as a result,

3. She never had to seriously consider taking the corporate jobs that her father made her feel as if she had to take.

Obviously, not every challenge is going to work out as neatly as Danielle's did for her. But the concept to remember here is that by Danielle carefully and honestly mining and then re-mining her *Gold*, she came up with a new, exciting employment option: becoming a television-production sales executive.

Your *Take-Away:*

It is essential as you go through *The 7 Steps of Emotion Mastery* for you to mine *Your Gold* and *Truth*. When you go through this process, in many instances, new ideas, paths, and solutions can be found or created.

The Importance of Being *Consequence Cognizant*— Identifying Some of Your Most Potent *Gold*

As we have discussed, knowing what you truly *don't* want in your life and what you abhor, fear, and are ashamed of is some of your most very motivating and powerful *Gold*. Therefore, identifying in each potential life-choice-making instance what the horrible, destructive, heinous consequences of a particular life choice can/will be is essential. We call the process of carefully identifying, absorbing, and considering all of the relevant results and outcomes of your choices and acts being *Consequence Cognizant*.

As we will discuss in more depth later, we are a quick-fix society. Our pop culture teaches us to always seek immediate gratification. It also reinforces the concept of getting what you want *without* considering the very real consequences of your acts. This highly flawed philosophy can absolutely lead you to make devastatingly destructive life choices. To illustrate what an absolutely horrible turn your life can take when you don't consider the consequences of your choices and actions, let's discuss the case of "John":

John was the main anchorman at a top-market West Coast television station. He appeared to have a tremendously rewarding career ahead of him. He had a talented, smart, and beautiful wife; a beautiful family; and journalism awards galore. He was well respected in his community and in the broadcasting business. In short, John was blessed with many gifts and seemingly had everything going for him.

But notwithstanding all of this, John felt compelled to allegedly commit illegal and highly ill-advised acts. Allegedly, all of this was done when John was overcome with great anger. As a direct result, John lost his coveted job over having allegedly committed these acts; risked destroying his broadcasting career for all-time; and received horrendous negative publicity. On the other hand, if John had been *Consequence Cognizant*—that is, if he had identified and appreciated all of the potential HORRENDOUS CONSEQUENCES of his choices and actions—I truly believe that he never would have committed any of his alleged acts and instead would have opted to preserve the exceedingly blessed life that he so very much enjoyed. Here are some of the potentially devastating consequences that he could have identified *before* he acted:

1. the loss of his wonderful and cherished career;

2. the loss of his great, coveted, stimulating, prestigious job;

3. the loss of tremendous, guaranteed income;

4. being the direct cause of tremendous embarrassment to his loving and wonderful wife and family;

5. living in ignominy;

6. being accused of committing a felony;

7. being convicted of committing a felony;

8. enduring the tremendous, unhealthy stress of having to go through all of these devastating consequences; and, possibly worst of all,

9. serving a sentence in jail!

The key here is that whenever you are faced with making an important life choice, *always* be *Consequence Cognizant*. Effectively implementing this process would most certainly have benefited individuals such as John Edwards, Tiger Woods, and Eliot Spitzer. Additionally, *always* keep in mind Warren Buffett's astute observation: "It can take twenty years [for you] to build a [good/great] reputation, and five minutes [for you] to destroy it!" Mr. Buffett's insight applies just as compellingly to the destruction of a blessed life as a result of making a self-destructive, emotion-filled choice.

Let's now discuss the case of "Audrey" in an anecdote that illustrates the (potential) benefits of her being *Consequence Cognizant*:

Audrey has never been very disciplined. Oftentimes she will put off doing things that would maintain or enhance her well-being until the very last moment—or not do them at all. Audrey's response to those who care about her and are lovingly exasperated by her lack of attention and consideration when it comes to those things that should be important to her is perhaps not surprising:

"If I don't do it today, tomorrow (or next week) is fine."

At nearly eighty-eight years old, Audrey, a widow of ten years, is still mentally sharp, and she remains a voracious reader of books, newspapers, and magazines that enlighten her regarding all sorts of subjects. She also spends time each day doing crossword puzzles and engaging in other, various intellectual pursuits. When I asked Audrey why she is so atypically disciplined in this area, she explains with great focus and fervor:

"Many individuals in my family have developed Alzheimer's and dementia at a relatively early age. It's *tragic* for them and for those who love them. I want to do *everything* I can to not get Alzheimer's, or at least do what I can to slow down its onslaught. I *absolutely don't* want to be a burden to my children."

In this instance, being acutely cognizant of the terrifying consequences of being stricken with Alzheimer's/dementia (some of her most very potent *Gold*) has broken Audrey's behavioral scripting of being undisciplined. Instead of following her normal course, because of her profound fear of getting Alzheimer's and the abhorrent thought of being a major burden to her children, Audrey consciously chooses to make positive life choices in this area, and some highly beneficial behavior modifications are the sweet result.

Your *Take-Aways:*

1. It is absolutely essential for you to carefully consider the consequences of your choices and acts *before* you make your life choices.

2. Identifying the most wonderful or most horrible, abhorrent, and heinous consequences of a life choice can be (among) your most potent pieces of *Gold* and/or *Truth* and can be one of your very strongest motivators in making a *Golden* and/or *Truthful* life choice.

STEP 2

Be Anticipatory: Effectively Anticipate That You Will Have to Make Certain Future, *Conscious* Life Choices

A large part of *Your Killer Emotions* is about acknowledging that in some number of years, months, weeks, or days from now, you will be called upon to make a *conscious* life choice at some future *Crunch Time!*... and that you will be thoroughly prepared to make—and will make—a *Golden* and *Truthful* choice. Before we move on to developing the art of being anticipatory, let's focus on the concepts of the *conscious* life choice.

The *Conscious* Life Choice

The reason why we focus on and so highly value the *conscious* life choice is because as human beings, as we have discussed, we have the ability to clearly think, reason, and evaluate *before* we make our choices and thereafter act, or refrain from acting. This is what you will strive to do in all of your life-choice-making opportunities.

Life choices are your all-important opportunities to lift and enhance your life, or, in the alternative, to diminish or destroy it. The quality of your life is a direct result of how you perceive, approach, and make your choices. As you endeavor to make your choices, you may well have to deal with one or more intense, toxic-emotion-generated energy charges that have the potential to cloud your best judgment and lead you to make self-defeating or self-sabotaging decisions. For example, you are married, and the situation presents itself (e.g., a business trip) whereby someone to whom you are not married, but to whom you are *incredibly* attracted/"crazy about," wants to have a fling with you. You have never before cheated on your spouse. However, at this moment in time, everything seems "so right" in following/succumbing to your seemingly overwhelming urge to "go for it." Therefore, you are faced with the choice of remaining faithful to and maintaining the trust of your spouse or having an affair/fling because it may be something you've fantasized about, and you imagine it would be incredibly exciting.

This was the case with "Drew" and "Melissa." Drew, 36, was a highly respected accountant for a major accounting firm. At the time, he was married and had two children. He had been with his firm for twelve years. Melissa, 24, was a recently hired assistant at the firm.

It was common knowledge at the firm that office romances and affairs were strongly frowned upon by the board of directors. However, one sultry summer evening at a firm retreat, Drew was overcome and emotionally hijacked by his sexual urges, as he and Melissa got together for a torrid night of sex. Drew engaged in this behavior even though he *knew* that he was under serious consideration to be made a partner at his firm—a position that he *very much* wanted and had worked tirelessly for years to secure.

Somehow Melissa's husband found out about the one-nighter and, in a rage, called Drew's wife and two of the firm's top board members to tell them about it. As a result of the situation becoming public and extremely uncomfortable for everyone at the firm, Drew was not made a partner. And soon thereafter, he was told to leave the firm. At about the same time, Drew's wife filed for divorce and sole custody of their children. He never saw Melissa again.

At the end of the day (or evening, as it were), Drew was left with *nothing*. A few days after leaving his firm, with intellectual clarity restored, he realized how he had ruined his life—for a one-evening affair.

The point of this story is that whenever you make a life choice, your goal is to have the intellectual clarity to *consciously* choose to make:

1. a *Golden* life choice that reflects, is consistent with, and enables you to attain *Your Gold*; and/or

2. a *Truthful* life choice that reflects, is consistent with, and enables you to live *Your Truth*.

In the story above, Drew's most cherished *Gold* was to become a partner at his firm. Obviously, by allowing his sexual urge to dismantle his best judgment at *Crunch Time!*, he made a self-sabotaging life choice that was totally inconsistent with his long-term *Gold*.

For our purposes, when we use the term "life choice," we will assume that if you make a *Golden* and/or *Truthful* one, you will follow through and act consistently with that decision.

Many people dislike making serious decisions to the extent that they avoid doing so as much as possible. But starting today, it is your goal to make the very most of each and every opportunity to make a *Golden* and/or a *Truthful* life choice.

The other day, I heard someone define choices as "giving up something you want for something you want [that motivates you] *more!*"[C] Implicit in this statement is that the person making the choice:

1. can think clearly and sabotaging-emotion-free; and there-fore, he or she

2. can effectively weigh his or her *competing values*, so that he or she

3. can *consciously* make a choice that accurately reflects his or her purest *Gold* and *Truth*.

From now on, this is how you can view the process according to which you will make all of your choices.

Your *Take-Aways:*

1. A life choice consists of two or more options.

2. Your goal when making a life choice is to think clearly and sabotaging-emotion-free; you can then consciously make a well thought-out choice that reflects your purest *Gold* and *Truth*.

Come Up BIG!—When It Counts the Most

An essential component of making highly beneficial life choices is to *Come Up Big!* when it counts the most.

As you know, there are certain daily choices that you make that won't mean much in the grand scheme of things and others that are life-changing. For example, for an athlete, there are matches and events that are truly "defining moments"; they have far more effect and impact on her/his career, potential earnings, growth, and legacy than others.

Similarly, for you there are life-choice-making outcomes involving certain individuals, things, and events that you value far more than others. As a result, it is essential for you to do your very best emotion-mastery work when the *Gold* and *Truth* at stake are *the* most important to you. With these thoughts in mind, it is essential, as you move forward, to as effectively as possible:

1. mine your most potent *Gold* and *Truth*; and thereby

2. identify the people, things, and events you value *above all others*; and

3. be as skillful as possible at *Crunch Time!* in order to *Come Up BIG!* when it counts *the most* by making a life choice that enables you to attain and live your *most* cherished *Gold* and *Truth*, respectively.

Your *Take-Away:*

Strive to identify what or whom you value the very most, for your goal is to make every effort to *Come Up BIG!* at *Crunch Time!* when your most prized *Gold* and *Truth* are at stake.

The Art of Being Anticipatory

For us, being anticipatory requires the recognition that at some point in the future, you will be asked to make a life choice during which you may well have to deftly navigate a barrage of competing and conflicting, highly charged emotions that have overwhelmed and/or sabotaged you in the past and/or have the very strong potential to do so in the future.

Let's spend some time discussing "general" and "specific" antici-pation and how they differ. To help illustrate and elucidate what you need to know, let me tell you about "Michael":

Michael is a very giving, open, warm soul who moved to Los Angeles from Chicago a few years ago. Unfortunately, Michael either attracts or is drawn to women who could be described as non-giving "takers."

Michael explained to me that there was a love interest of his, "Christi," who had just gone through a horrible two-year divorce. Throughout this long, arduous process, Michael was there for Christi as a friend, an advisor, a confidante, and a shoulder to cry on. He was essentially there for her in every way. Over those two years, Michael would take Christi to fun dinners, to the movies, to the theatre, and on various other outings. Michael did all of this in the true spirit of wanting to help and to be there for his longtime friend, Christi, in the present, while hoping that he could build a romantic relationship with her at some point in the future. During this time, Christi repeatedly told Michael that she looked forward to the day when her divorce was finalized so that they could spend time together, go away on romantic trips, and possibly share a life. During the last few months prior to Christi's divorce, she would hold Michael's hand, give him long hugs, and even, on occasion, passionately kiss him—all of which Michael loved and very much looked forward to.

Finally, Christi secured her divorce, but soon thereafter, she began talking about "starting her new life," "finally being independent," "being able to date again," and "wanting to discover herself again." Christi's new, startling and jarring, independence-seeking mindset manifested itself as a jolting reality in which the daily phone conversations between them (the great majority of which had been initiated by Christi) suddenly became a thing of the past. When she did call Michael, inevitably it was to suggest that they go out to dinner, meaning that she wanted Michael to take her to an expensive L.A. restaurant—the type of date that he could easily afford and had, up until that point, been more than happy to pay for.

As time wore on, Michael almost never heard from Christi, and when they did speak, she would no longer tell him how much she missed him, how much she appreciated the person he was, or how much she enjoyed his company. Instead, she would simply say: "I haven't gone out for a really great dinner since I last saw you! We should get together and go out!"

For a while, Michael felt and acted like Pavlov's dog. In spite of how used, angry, and rejected he felt, whenever Michael heard Christi's sweet voice (the potentially toxic stimulus), he immediately visualized her beautiful face and smile. He remembered the very good times they had shared during the two-year period when she was securing her divorce. He pictured and was "addicted" to such things as the feeling of his lips on hers and the touch of her skin. He couldn't get her scent out of his mind. As a result, Michael's intellect and best judgment went absolutely MIA whenever he had any interaction with Christi—so much so, in fact, that as soon as Christi suggested dinner, he'd jump at the chance and was ready, once again, to give her the world.

When I asked Michael to describe his thoughts and feelings during this highly frustrating time, he said, "You know, when she needed me during those two tough years, I thought we could have the perfect life together. But now, there are times when all I want to do is tell Christi that I'm angry and feel used, because as soon as she doesn't need me anymore emotionally, she drops me like a hot potato . . . except, of course, when she wants to go to a trendy restaurant. Then she calls me! But every time she calls, and I hear her voice and think about all of the great things about her, I lose my head and my nerve. I completely [emotionally] cave! I'm so afraid that if I confront her, she'll just never call me again. So, I immediately invite her out to dinner or to a play, hoping that *this* time, we can somehow reestablish what we had prior to her divorce . . . but it never happens. As soon as the dinner's over, there's no traction whatsoever! She's gone for months. I *absolutely hate my weakness*! I feel like such a spineless idiot! And it seems so ironic, because I'm so rational in every other area of my life!"

As we move forward, it is important to understand that the manner in which Michael acted with Christi was not an isolated case. Instead it was part of a poisonous, sabotaging behavioral pattern—a destructive, emotion-triggered script caused by Michael's emotional hijacking at *Crunch Time!*. Giving everything he could to every woman at the beginning of every romantic encounter left Michael feeling "taken for granted" or "used" when these women wouldn't or couldn't respond to him in kind or on his timetable. This was a "general" problem for Michael, and not just one specifically related to Christi.

After some honest and insightful conversations between us, as well as some effective self-exploration by Michael, he could see how to be both "generally" and "specifically" anticipatory at *Crunch Time!* regarding his future dating choices and behavior. In the case of Christi, there was a *specific* (positive) history, with *specific* memories, feelings, emotions, and urges that were triggered whenever Michael and Christi would speak or meet. These stimuli would consistently derail Michael's thought processes, best judgment, and his best-laid plans at *Crunch Time!*. As a result, Michael *specifically* knew what to anticipate when he would next speak with Christi. He knew what the *specific* landmines would be and exactly where they would be. He could *specifically* anticipate Christi's mellifluous voice and its tone, her manner, and the approach she would take when she would next suggest that they get together at a hot restaurant or plan dinner and a play. By being able to anticipate the very *specific* Christi stimuli that he would be presented with, and by being able to acknowledge how his emotions had overpowered and negated his best judgment in the past, Michael would be able to *anticipate* his future choices and *prepare specific* actions and responses for when he would next talk to her. The clear aim of *The Prevent Offense* would be to prevent him from making another poisonous, energy-charge-flooded, self-sabotaging, self-esteem-deflating, highly frustrating life choice involving Christi.

However, Michael also recognized that he has a *general* pattern of folding like a house of cards in the wind whenever pretty, seductive women initially pay attention to him—regardless of whether they continue to be attentive, caring, giving, and/or loving down the road. As a result, he needs to be *generally* anticipatory. Michael must also anticipate the choices he will make when he is dealing with attractive women whom he doesn't yet know. Essentially, he needs to develop *general* anticipatory strategies to cover situations for which he doesn't have specific data.

Your own anticipation can also be either *general* or *specific* depending upon whether the life choice you want to make is resolute or flexible. Here's why: If your choice is to smoke or not smoke; drink or not drink; eat fattening foods or decline them; or perform some act that clearly enhances your life or, conversely, diminishes it, your choice may well be crystal-clear, and your anticipatory response that you prepare can be *specific*. However, there are times when, depending upon the situation, people, and/or consequences involved, you will need to be more adaptable and therefore prepare a more flexible form of anticipation.

So, in instances when you can anticipate the *specific* options and values that will enter your life-choice equation at *Crunch Time!*, you can decide ahead of time where and when to be resolute; however, when you don't know or have enough specific data, this may well call for a more flexible approach on your part. I often advise clients: If you can *specifically* anticipate what a future choice will involve, you can write what choice you'll make at *Crunch Time!* in pen; if you can't, you'd best be advised to use pencil instead.

For example, you may choose to decline desserts, except when it's a very special occasion, such as your child's birthday. You may decide ahead of time that *this* is one of those infrequent occasions for which you will make an allowance and take a break from your diet and say, "Yes, thank you," to a small slice of cake. But be clear, *this will be a choice that you have previously thought through and made with no potentially poisonous emotions or temptations clouding your best judgment.* Your most precious *Gold*—to continue to lose weight or stay slim—remains; however, this flexibility acknowledges that there will be times when a slight deviation from *Your Gold* and *Your Truth* doesn't threaten your original plan and primary goal.

When exploring *ironclad* versus variable/flexible life choices, it is important to keep the concepts of *specific* and *general* anticipation in mind. For example, if you can *specifically* anticipate what individuals, entities, or occurrences will call for you to make a certain life choice, you can far more easily make ironclad life choices ahead of *Crunch Time!.* And, because there may be a number of *specific* stimuli that you can predict will trigger or enter into your life choice, you can make various ironclad choices ahead of time regarding each one— even if they are different depending upon the person, entity, or occasion involved.

However, if you don't have enough *specifics*, and as a result, you can't specifically anticipate what variables or options will be presented to you at *Crunch Time!*, you have three courses of action that you can choose to take:

1. Make an *ironclad* choice no matter who or what is involved. For example: "I'm NOT going out this weekend, no matter who asks me out!, because I need to hunker down and catch up on my work" (*Specific* anticipation, with an ironclad, predetermined life choice.);

2. Make a choice to not go out this weekend unless a certain desirable person asks you out. For example, "I'm not going

out this weekend, except if Brad asks me. For him and *only* for him, I'll put off my studying until the following weekend, as Brad's going to be out of town then!" (*Specific* anticipation, with two ironclad, predetermined life choices.) In this scenario, you have made ironclad choices depending upon your valuation of the circumstances in the context of the individuals involved or possibly involved; or

3. Make a choice not to go out this weekend unless someone comes along who piques your interest, and that someone is exciting *enough* to merit reworking your study schedule. (*General* anticipation, with more flexibility regarding your choice.)

These forms of strategic *specific* and *general* anticipation are analogous to athletic preparation. If you know whom you are playing against and/or you have competed against them before, you have *specific knowledge* of their strategies, weaknesses, and predispositions. It has been said that the greatest predictor of future behavior is past behavior. Assuming this is true, you can create a *specific* game plan in anticipation of *specific* things taking place. However, if you don't know whom you will be competing against and/or have no history with them—as well as no means to secure any relevant information regarding them—you need to be anticipatory in a more *general* way, as there are likely to be many more unknowns and variables involved. Therefore, the game plan that you construct will need to be more flexible and adaptable, as there will be emotions, urges, impulses, and pulls that you might not expect and that you will need to deal with appropriately and effectively.

Years ago, I heard an ESPN Radio interview with the highly successful, former USC football coach Pete Carroll, who was talking about how the USC football team would prepare for their upcoming big games. In pertinent part, Coach Carroll discussed *general* and *specific* anticipation. This is essentially what he said:

> "We always prepare for the known [the *specific*] and the unknown [the *general*]. Often it's how you handle the unknown that will determine your success. We always practice [prepare] well. This gives us the best chance to deal effectively with both the known and the unknown."

According to Coach Carroll, if you prepare correctly and thoroughly, the chances are far greater that you will act and react most effectively at *Crunch Time!* to both the things and events that you can specifically anticipate and to those you can't.

As you develop your *Prevent Offense*, one way for you to be *specifically* anticipatory is to prepare a list of *ironclad* life choices that you will make regarding specific individuals, events, and things when the appropriate opportunities present themselves.

Here's a sample *Specific Anticipation List*:

1. I will NOT! make any choices or act when I'm angry.

2. I will NOT! spend time with friends on Sundays, as I need to spend quality time with my son/daughter.

3. I will NEVER! have more than one drink if I have to drive later.

4. When Christi calls and says that we should have dinner, my answer will be, "NO, THANK YOU." Let her grow to appreciate me and my company more than she does now. And if she doesn't, then it's no real loss, anyway!

5. Even though I love salt, the doctor says it's POISON! for someone with blood pressure as high as mine. So from now on, I will NO LONGER put salt in my food or eat foods high in salt.

6. No matter how tempting, I will NOT be intimate with Sam tonight.

7. Even if I'm tired in the morning, at least four times a week, I WILL exercise before work.

8. No matter how many invitations I receive from my friends to go shopping, I will say NO! I need to save my money this year to pay for math and English tutoring for my daughter/son.

In all of these cases, you anticipate that you will be called upon to make life choices in connection with the nuggets of *Gold* and *Truth* identified above. By making your *Specific Anticipation List,*[7] you take a significant step in clearly acknowledging that when you are called upon to make a future life choice regarding certain individuals, events, opportunities, or options, you will *know* exactly what choice to make at *Crunch Time!.* Your goal is to have the relevant, pre-made life choice cognitively click in and guide you at *Crunch Time!,* so that you can make a life choice that is consistent with the one you prepared during your *Prevent Offense.*

---

7 You can download this and all other *Lists* from the Web site for *Your Killer Emotions* (www.yourkilleremotions.com).

Your *Take-Aways:*

1. Being anticipatory calls for you to look into the future and contemplate both:

   a. the emotion-generated, energy-charged challenges you may be faced with at *Crunch Time!*; and

   b. what you will do in a given life-choice situation.

2a. We focus on two categories of anticipation: *specific* and *general.* You can utilize *specific* anticipation when you can anticipate, with specificity, what stimuli you will be exposed to when making a future life choice. If you cannot specifically anticipate what or whom you will be confronted with, you can utilize the strategy of *general* anticipation. This usually calls for you to have more flexibility with your responses at *Crunch Time!*.

2b. Essentially, when you have *specific* knowledge regarding someone, something, or an upcoming event because of past experience or research that you have done, oftentimes you can *specifically anticipate* what you will be faced with at *Crunch Time!* and, therefore, what choice you will (want to) make at that time. However, if you lack *specific* knowledge of the individuals, things, or events involved, it is far more likely that you will rely on *general anticipation* at *Crunch Time!*.

3. Preparing a *Specific Anticipation List* of future life choices that you want to make regarding certain people, things, and events can be very helpful in enabling you to make *Golden* and *Truthful* life choices at *Crunch Time!*.

Event Visualization

Now, let's take a moment to discuss and absorb the process of *event visualization*. It is well known that many athletes frequently take quiet time prior to and in preparation for an athletic encounter in order to *visualize* certain scenarios that they anticipate could present themselves when they're on the court/field. By way of illustration, let me share with you some relevant parts of my pre-match preparation when I was to play my first exhibition tennis match against Arthur Ashe the year before he became the world's number-one men's tennis player:

> I had known for weeks that I was going to play a match against Arthur in my hometown of Brooklyn, New York to benefit The United Negro College Fund. At the time, I was the number-one singles player on the Harvard University tennis team and had captured such titles as the Men's Eastern Singles Championship.
>
> Fortunately for me, when I was in Miami Beach two weeks before our exhibition match, Arthur played a match there that I was able to carefully watch, study, and take notes on. The following week, I saw Arthur play on TV, and I was able to learn even more about and further confirm certain patterns of his game. As a direct result, I was able to very *specifically visualize* what shots Arthur was most comfortable hitting in a given situation. For example, if an opponent approached the net on Arthur's excellent backhand, he almost always responded with a down-the-line shot.
>
> After watching Arthur play two full matches, and with many of his shot patterns or preferences etched in my mind, each day, for an hour or so during the week before our match, I *visualized* what shots I would hit to Arthur and then *visualized* his responses. I would then lock these *event visualizations* into my mind so that I could instantly access them during the match.

Because I was able to effectively:

1. *specifically anticipate* what to expect from Arthur in a given situation;

2. instantaneously access my pre-determined responses at *Crunch Time!* (during the heat of the match); and

3. execute my pre-determined *event-visualization* game plan, on that day, I was able to secure my sweetest athletic achievement: I defeated Arthur, 6–4.

What the above story points out is that during *Step 2* of your *Prevent Offense*:

1. you acknowledge that you will be called upon at some point in the future—*Crunch Time!*—to make a life choice;

2. you will *specifically* or *generally anticipate* the choice that you will make at *Crunch Time!* given the specific or general circumstances presented to you; and

3. you will lock this *event visualization* (your pre-determined choice[s]) into your mind so that you are instantaneously able to cognitively access the appropriate *visualizations* (your choice[s]) at *Crunch Time!*.

Next, play out in your mind your actually making your *Golden* and *Truthful* choice(s). *Visualize* this over and over again. Remember, this is how you fervently aspire to act. Then experience, celebrate, and savor how very good—or great!—it will *feel* to make a life choice that enables and empowers you to attain *Your Gold*, live *Your Truth*, and own and create your future. This is accomplished by knowing what you truly want to attain and what you want to be; and by tapping into the *PETS* that motivate and catalyze you to "do it" and "be it." Let these wonderful feelings travel through and become embedded in your *Heart-of-Hearts*[8] (your heart, mind, and psyche) as you recognize the sweet gifts and blessings ahead.

Next, lock these exhilarating feelings—these highly potent energy charges—deep within your *Heart-of-Hearts*. You will then be able to tap into these highly potent, positive energy charges and channel them into your *Frisual*™ (which we will discuss in the next *Step*) at *Crunch Time!*.

Your *Take-Away:*

At *Crunch Time!*, you will be called upon to access, replay, and utilize the *visualizations* of potential life choices that you have locked into your mind during this *Step* of *The Prevent Offense*.

For us, another component of being *anticipatory* is objectively and freely *acknowledging* that you have made self-defeating and/or self-sabotaging life choices in the past. This calls for you to honestly and non-defensively look back and examine instances in your past when you made self-sabotaging and self-esteem-lowering life choices:

1. because your choices weren't well thought-out;

2. because your emotions clouded your best judgment; and/or

3. because of some other decision-making breakdown or flaw.

The beautiful thing about your past mistakes is that you can learn from them; objectively understand what went wrong or was flawed; equip yourself with a better, more evolved, and more efficacious skill set; assimilate all of this data; and secure a sweet, well thought-out

---

8 We will focus on the concept of your *Heart-of-Hearts* in our discussion of *Step 4*.

life-choice triumph your next time out—which is what you will be thoroughly *prepared* to do!

So, in preparation for a future life-choice opportunity, review and think through what went awry the last time a potentially self-defeating and/or self-destructive option was presented to you, and you chose to take it. Then take time to decide what will be a more constructive and/or beneficial way to handle a similar life-choice opportunity the next time.

Here are some examples of hypothetical inner conversations that acknowledge a flawed life choice being made in the past and identify a more effectively thought-out *Gold-* and *Truth*-attaining strategy in anticipation of similar future life-choice opportunities being presented to you:

1. "The last time I was offered too much alcohol at a party/at dinner, I continued drinking because I wanted to be social, and it seemed harmless at the time. That lapse in judgment resulted in my getting a DUI, and I lost my license. This was devastating to me in so many ways. It was awful.

   Next time, after one drink, I will resolutely say, 'NO, THANKS!' I don't want to risk the unthinkable consequences should I lose my license again, and this time, permanently! Nor do I want to risk the much worse consequence of injuring my children, myself, or someone else should I get into an accident while driving drunk!"

2. "The last time that I had a relatively lucrative, ego-gratifying position offered to me by a competing firm, I accepted it without truly considering the (profound) consequences. Because of the rigorous demands of the job, my children were raised, pretty much, by revolving nannies. I now regretfully realize that this caused my children to feel unloved, unwanted, and undervalued. All terrible things!

Four years later, with my children having various disciplinary problems and related challenges, I have quit my job in order to be with them. The next time that any other similarly demanding position is offered or becomes available, I will respond with an absolute, 'NO, THANK YOU!' My children's emotional security is far more important than some extra financial security or some hollow job title."

3. "The last time my mother told me how I should be living my life, I shot back in vitriolic anger, telling her what a terrible, selfish parent she had been . . . and then I stormed out the door.

My children and I haven't seen or spoken with her in over a year. I don't want to have this horrible rift with my mom, and I certainly don't want to deprive my children of experiencing and enjoying their only grandma. But somehow, she *always* knows how to push my buttons, whether she means to or not.

It's my mom's birthday next week, and I've told my dad that we'd like to celebrate it with her. And *this* time, because I want to have a loving, or at least a civil, relationship with my mom, and I want my children to know and enjoy the love of their grandma, I'm prepared to not let *anything* my mom says or does bother me. I must and will be the peacemaker from now on!"

So, let's do a review here. In all three of the above inner conversations, there is an *acknowledgment* by the person in issue of past life-choice-making faux pas and the *development* of both a revised and a significantly more beneficial game plan to implement in the future. The aim of these *Steps* is to secure a far more desirable result the next time a life choice involving a particular stimulus is presented.

Your *Take-Away:*

It is important for you to *acknowledge* a past life-choice-making mistake so that you can develop an appropriate and a more beneficial game plan for future, similar life-choice-making opportunities.

STEP 3

Construct Your Future *Frisuals*™

The strategic process by which you will consistently make *Golden* and *Truthful* life choices is called *Frisualization*™, and the vehicle for taking you to where you want to go is the *Frisual*™.

As a means of studying how *you* will inevitably lead and compel yourself to make positive, spirit-lifting life choices, let's now discuss an essential concept and component of this process.

Pushing Your Own *Personal Emotional Triggers (Your PETS)*

In many ways, *Your Killer Emotions* is about *YOU*:

1. *identifying* your strongest, most super-charged *PETS*; and

2. using these *PETS* to motivate, drive, and compel you to make life choices that will enable you to attain *Your Gold* and live *Your Truth*.

You've heard of one person pushing another person's (emotional) buttons. It's now time for *you* to identify and *consciously* and *purposefully* push your own emotional buttons as a means to motivate yourself to make great life choices. This is, in every sense of the word, true self-motivation and self-help.

Let me give you some illustrations of how I and others have pushed our own *Personal Emotional Triggers*—our *PETS*—in order to motivate us to attain our goals:

BULLETIN-BOARD MATERIAL

1. There is a very well-known and exceedingly successful actress who, early on in her career, sought representation at a very successful, top-tier talent agency. As the story goes, she was summarily rejected by way of a cold form letter from that agency, in essence telling her that she just didn't have what it takes to make it in the acting business. Since that terribly deflating day ten years ago, however, this individual has become a *huge* success. She has also told many people that she keeps that rejection letter posted on her bulletin board, as it motivates her everyday to show everyone that she indeed does have what it takes to be a major star! She says it also fuels her to remain hungry and focused and to stay on top of her game.

   Similarly, on Colin Cowherd's national radio show, I heard pro-football expert Sal Paolantonio being interviewed about why the mega-star quarterback and the coach of the New England Patriots—Tom Brady and Bill Belichick, respectively—have been able to win with such remarkable consistency, year after year. Mr. Paolantonio said, "The rocket fuel of this country is [the feeling of] resentment. Brady was passed over [in the NFL draft]. Belichick was [greatly] underrated." My take on Mr. Paolantonio's observation is that the *huge* feelings of resentment that both Tom Brady and Bill Belichick allegedly harbor within fuel, motivate, and catalyze them to give their very best efforts each and every week in an attempt to (continue) to prove all of their detractors wrong! They are accomplishing this by masterfully pushing their own emotional buttons, with their *Gold* being the attainment of professional greatness and Super Bowl rings.

2. My mom has a tremendous number of very positive traits. Unfortunately, finishing projects that she starts hasn't been one of them. Either she has found a way to be defeated by a setback or has become a "victim" as the result of some negative occurrence, and she soon thereafter abandons her project; or she has striven for (unattainable) perfection. As a sad result, she has perceived that nothing she does is good enough, so she has often failed to complete what she so brilliantly envisions. Obviously, both of these are highly self-sabotaging and self-esteem-diminishing behavioral scripts.

   It pains me deeply to witness how extraordinarily talented my mom is, yet she rarely tastes the sweet success of seeing her great ideas become completed realities. My mom's self-sabotaging behavior in this area strikes a primal chord deep within my psyche. Seeing her not take advantage of her gifts and efforts, time after time, triggers huge, high-voltage energy charges within me, and in reaction, I use tenacious focus and discipline to complete every project I truly value. Essentially, the thought and vision of my mom, *once again*, failing to finish something quite wonderful that she starts motivates and compels me NOT to emulate her behavior or suffer her profound disappointments!

Her self-sabotaging behavior motivates me to make sure
that I cross the finish line!

3. As we discussed earlier, I am someone who *hates* being in
a hospital if I'm the patient. I will do *anything* and *change
any behavior*! to avoid being operated on for an illness or a
health-related problem. This thought and visualization truly
scare me to death! So this *fear* in this area is one of my most
potent, energy-charged *PETS*. I also cherish my health and
general well-being above almost anything else. (This *PET*
is way high up on my *Gold List*.) I developed this health-
focused outlook from my dad, who always took excellent
care of himself, ate sensibly, and got lots of exercise and rest.
The combination of these highly constructive behaviors
and his sturdy genetic endowment enabled my dad to live a
healthy and vital life until he passed away at the age of 100
years and two months. He continued to work and love his
position at T. J. Maxx until he was past the age of ninety-
eight.

I, as an admiring son and fan, want to do everything that
I can to replicate my dad's wonderful health and extraordinary, long and active life. One obstacle for me is that I have
always truly loved fried foods. And they were a regular part
of my daily diet until the day I visited a friend of the family
in the hospital. He was in his fifties, about to have his second
major bypass surgery after suffering a second heart attack.
He was obviously scared to death that he might not survive
the operation and never again be with his loving wife, his
beautiful children, and his adoring mother. Seeing this man
cooped-up in the hospital room and absolutely terrified, as
the nurses readied him for surgery, shook me to my core.

His wife whispered to me, "'Ben' has severely clogged
arteries, and he never watched what he ate. He thought that

he was indestructible." She spoke of him in the past tense, as her eyes welled up with tears. I will never forget the scene of Ben's wife and mother doing everything they could to seem optimistic and uplifting when talking to Ben just before he was to be sedated, and then leaving the room and breaking down into inconsolable tears, convinced that they would never see Ben alive again!

The nurses then wheeled Ben off to surgery, and I left the room. After saying goodbye to everyone, I immediately asked myself:

"Do I want the *momentary pleasure* of tasting fried food at the risk of ending up like Ben? Do I want to be cooped-up—TOTALLY VULNERABLE—and at the mercy of doctors and nurses who may or may not be qualified or on their 'A games' that day when I *so* need them to be? Do I want to be absolutely SCARED TO DEATH as I await a potential life-ending surgery? And, do I want to keep eating fried foods and potentially IRREPARABLY DAMAGE MY HEART, so that I seriously risk not enjoying the long, vital, active life I crave?"

OR...

"Do I want to say an emphatic, 'NO, THANK YOU!' to fried foods from now on and hopefully NEVER face heart (or any other related) surgery?!"

I then visualized myself in a hospital bed like Ben, awaiting surgery, scared beyond belief that I will NEVER, EVER SEE OR BE WITH MY LOVED ONES AGAIN! I also visualized the deep pain and angst that I would put the ones who love me through should I need to undergo such surgery or die during or soon after surgery simply because I wasn't disciplined enough to refrain from eating fried foods.

The collective energy charges from this thought process and these visualizations were so extraordinarily powerful that they totally negated any competing energy charges that were generated from the good taste of and momentary pleasure I received from eating fried foods. They totally decimated them! As a result, at *Crunch Time!*, whenever I am faced with eating a fried food, I am able to tap into one of my very strongest *PETS*. I am able to think and value clearly, and I am thrilled to be able to say that I can count on one hand the number of times over the past twenty-five years that I have eaten something fried.

The key here is for you to absorb and embrace that:

1. there are certain *PETS* that evoke supremely strong energy charges within you; and

2. by skillfully pushing *your own* emotional buttons (*Your PETS*), you can motivate and empower yourself to make *Golden* and *Truthful* life choices.

Your *Take-Away*:

When faced with making an important life choice, you are wise to pursue the following truest and most constructive forms of self-help:

1. Identify your very strongest, most relevant *PETS*; and

2. Push your own emotional buttons so that you are supremely motivated and, as a result, inevitably led to make the most *Golden* and/or *Truthful* life choices.

O.K. Now that you have the concept of how you can push your own emotional buttons, let's go on to study *The Frisual*.

The *Frisual*™

A *Frisual* is the combination of two processes:

1. *Framing*™ the life choice or issue before you in such an artful and compelling way that you are supremely motivated and thereby inevitably led to make a life choice that enables you to attain *Your Gold* and live *Your Truth*; and

2. *Visualization*: *visualizing Your Gold* and/or *Your Truth*, whether before, during, or after you *Frame*™ the life choice or issue before you.

Let's first study the all-important concept of *Framing*. *Framing* is a process whereby you *Frame* your life choice—that is, you set it in a context that is *so* powerfully, emotionally charged and *agenda-driven* that you override the less potent energy charges generated by emotions and urges that could derail you at *Crunch Time!* You load up the choice before you with your most purely potent *PETS* so that you are energized to make a life choice consistent with and reflective of *Your Gold* and *Your Truth*.

As we study how to *Frame* your life choice, let me share with you my very personal story of how I discovered the concept of *Framing*, which I expect will illuminate how the process works:

While I was growing up, my dad worked six days a week and many late nights in order to support our family. Fortunately for me, my dad's hard work afforded my mom the opportunity to be at home with me most of the time. So during my early years, my mom essentially raised me. That's the good news. But because my mom was *always* there, as opposed to my dad, who never seemed to be there, I thought and felt that my mom loved and valued me and that my dad didn't. This caused me to feel totally rejected by my dad.

One very toxic result of all my rejection-based pain, hurt, and anger was that I would regularly sit in my room, watch TV, and gorge myself on cookies, candy, pudding, cheesecake, mac-and-cheese, and the like. As a direct result, I became a severely overweight child, with strong, deep feelings of insecurity, unlovability, anger, hurt, and low self-esteem. This profound problem was combined with the fact that my large-muscle coordination was slow to develop, so I was also exceedingly clumsy. Without a doubt, I was a real mess as a child.

When I was in the first grade, I developed a crush on a classmate of mine, a very cute girl named Dale. I carried this crush through the eighth grade. My big problem was that because I was so fat, (I perceived that) Dale didn't find me romantically attractive. As a result, I wasn't potential boyfriend material. So I chose to become the class clown, attempting to get Dale's attention with my jokes. However, the attention that I received as her "funny friend" was not the kind of attention that I longed for.

Along with all of this, I was always extremely frustrated about how fat I was and that I wasn't able to fit into the cool, tight white jeans that the other slim kids in my class were wearing. Trust me, there was nothing "cool" to be found in the "husky" departments or in the "big boy" stores in which I had to shop! I also *hated* people judgmentally watching what I ate (because I was fat).

Then one day, when I was about seven years old, my mom tripped on a broken curb and fell hard into the street, severely shattering her hip. She was forced to stay in the hospital for many weeks and undergo three separate operations in order to remedy the problem. This seemingly horrible turn of events, however, did have a silver lining for me. My dad needed to come home from work early each night and spend evenings with me. He also stopped working on weekends. The result of all this was that he took me with him to the local beach club on Saturdays and Sundays . . . , which I absolutely loved!

Throughout my dad's life, he had been a very good athlete. During our weekends together, I would sit and watch my dad play highly competitive matches of handball and paddleball with his friends. After that, my dad would give me a paddle (a wooden racquet), and he would throw balls to me; I, in turn, would try to hit them. At first, it was a disaster! With my coordination challenges, I barely made contact with the ball. But slowly, I started to improve. Some months later, my dad and I began to hit the ball gently and slowly against a handball/paddleball wall. My hand-eye coordination started to get a lot better, which made my dad happy; and that in turn made me happy, as I craved any bit of approval that I could garner from my dad.

The next problem for me was that when I needed to run to hit a ball, I was so fat and clumsy that I'd never get to the necessary spot in order to hit it on the fly or on the required first bounce. Even though running to that specific area on the court was very slow going (literally!), I'd try and try. Then, one Sunday when I was about nine years old, my dad and I watched a paddleball exhibition match between four top eleven-year-old boys. All of them were thin, fast, and agile. My dad's off-handed remarks about how good these boys were—especially his very positive appraisal of one very particularly fast and talented boy, Davey Klein—cut through me and hurt me right down to my core. I so very much wanted and needed my dad to feel that way about me!: to love me, approve of me, value me, respect me, and be proud of me! That night, I stuffed myself with ice cream, cookies, and macaroni-and-cheese, as intense feelings of hurt, rejection, and of just being plain "less than" and "not good enough" surged through me. I wanted and needed something to immediately make me feel better. And comfort food was always the quick fix!

It was soon after that very memorable low point that I had an epiphany. I realized, "If I can become a very good paddleball player, I will secure and truly *feel* the things that I *so very much want*: my dad's camaraderie, his attention, his approval, and his love." (My very purest and most potent *Gold!*) And I would be much more likely to accomplish this if I were faster and more agile . . . *which meant that I needed to lose weight!*

So, if I had thought to make my most potent *Gold List* at that time, first and foremost on that *List* (with a bullet) would have been:

1. ATTAINING AND FEELING MY DAD'S LOVE AND APPROVAL. (I wanted this more than *anything*!)

From that day on, I found an emotion—the LOVE that I craved from my dad—that was *so* emotionally charged, and therefore so energy-potent, that it overpowered and negated my previous energy-charged needs and urges to eat everything good-tasting in sight in an effort to temporarily assuage my deep feelings of hurt, rejection, anger, and hopelessness.

Essentially, from that point on, every time I was offered a fattening treat and had the opportunity to decline the offer, and thereby take an additional step toward losing weight, I would *Frame* the choice before me as follows:

"Do I want to eat something that will give me *momentary* pleasure (enjoying the taste of fattening food) and continue to:

1. FEEL ABSOLUTELY LOUSY ABOUT BEING FAT!;

2. FEEL ABSOLUTELY LOUSY ABOUT MYSELF!;

3. experience the HORRIBLE FEELING! I get when others make fun of me or give me disapproving looks when I eat; and

4. trigger and increase the DEBILITATING WEAKNESS! I feel as I continue to eat weight-increasing food, even though I *know* IT'S KILLING ME!;

OR...

Do I want to say an emphatic, 'NO, THANK YOU!' and thereafter resolutely decline eating the sabotaging food, and thereby seize the opportunity to become thinner in order for me to truly attain what I desire *far, far more* than anything else!:

1. the incomparably amazing feeling that MY DAD LOVES ME!;

2. the indescribable feeling that MY DAD APPROVES OF ME! and IS PROUD OF ME!; and

3. the incredible feeling that MY DAD IS CHOOSING TO SPEND TIME WITH ME! and play ball with me because HE TRULY ENJOYS IT and HE WANTS TO BE WITH ME?!"

I then added (or "piled on") the awesome energy charges generated by:

1. how absolutely HORRIBLE and ASHAMED I felt about how FAT I was; and

2. how PROFOUNDLY UNHAPPY I felt about the person I was.

By constructing this *Frame*, I was able to tap into and channel my most supremely potent bundle of energy charges from my most valued *PETS*. This combination of energy charges totally blew away any competing energy charges that had previously catalyzed me to make the self-sabotaging life choice to opt for the immediate gratification of eating fattening foods. As a result, I began to more and more consistently turn down candy, cake, cookies, and other sweets; and to my heartfelt exhilaration, I began to lose weight. A lot of weight!

Essentially, I was able to harness the tremendous energy charges triggered by the emotions of my dad's love, my shame, and my intense fear of never securing, and therefore not ever feeling, my dad's love and approval. These tremendous energy charges combined to overpower and thereby negate the urge to enjoy some quick-fix, fattening-food gratification. As a result, I was able to make life choices that reflected the clearly thought-out goals and dreams that I wanted to attain and enjoy, respectively.

Put another way: I found values—attaining my dad's love, approval, respect, and camaraderie—that motivated me *far more* than eating fattening foods did.

Soon thereafter, I identified two more precious pieces of *Gold* that would "make my heart sing":

1. I wanted to be thin enough so that DALE would view me as a potential BOYFRIEND; and

2. I wanted to be thin enough to fit into the COOL, thin-legged WHITE JEANS that my friends were wearing.

It was then that I came upon the tremendous potency of *visualizing* my *Gold*, along with constructing the most compelling, energy-charged *Frames*. I eventually called this combination a *Frisual*—or a *Frame*, plus a super-energy-charged *visual* of my *Gold* or *Truth* attainment.

So, from that time on, whenever there was any temptation/opportunity to go off my diet or regimen, I'd *Frisual*. My *Frame* would be:

"Do I want the momentary pleasure of eating the fattening food while continuing to be and feel like a 'FAT SLOB!'; to FEEL LOUSY! ABOUT WHO I AM and MY IMPOTENCY! to positively change my life; to NEVER! have or FEEL MY DAD'S LOVE; to NOT have any chance to BE DALE'S BOYFRIEND;

and, to NOT FIT INTO THE CLOTHES that I really want to wear?;

OR...

Do I RESOLUTELY DECLINE! the food/candy (which would hurt for only a second or two) but gain and really FEEL MY DAD'S LOVE! and HIS APPROVAL FOR A LIFETIME!; become the person I want to be and will feel GREAT! about; possibly BECOME DALE'S BOYFRIEND!; EUPHORI-CALLY! FIT INTO THE CLOTHES I'D LOVE TO WEAR!; and FEEL ABSOLUTELY AMAZ-ING! about my ability, through my making GREAT! LIFE CHOICES TO SO VERY POSITIVELY CHANGE MY LIFE?!"

Then I'd vividly *visualize* all of the beautiful positives that would come from my making a *Gold*-attaining choice (enjoying my dad's love; being Dale's boyfriend; fitting into the cool clothes that other kids could wear), along with all the horrible consequences that surely would result if I opted to eat fattening foods and continue being a "fat slob" or "fat pig"—which is how I felt about and saw myself.

When the choice was *Framed* and *visualized* in this manner, declining the sweets and treats was truly a piece of cake! There was no contest. For me, and for those whom I've counseled, it has been the energy-triggering *Frame*, along with the energy-charged *visual*, that have supplied the combined, one-two, highly potent energy punch that has knocked out the energy charges that had sabotaged us in the past. Therefore, our *Frisuals* enabled and empowered our intellect and best judgment to prevail.

As time went on and I lost weight, I'd make a habit of looking in the mirror and savoring "THE NEW ME!" As a byproduct of this, I'd commit to memory the *visual* of the "me" that was looking more and more like the person who I always wanted to be and had dreamt about becoming. I would then make sure that I would incorporate this incredibly positive-energy-charged picture into my future *visuals . . .* , which significantly increased their potency and effectiveness.

As I looked in the mirror, I made the effort to acknowledge my *Frisuals* and thoroughly enjoy the inspiring realization that I truly had the *ability* and the *power* to create for myself the life that I had always wanted. I then made sure that the huge emotion-generated energy charge from feeling this wonderful empowerment was channeled into and stored in my mind and my *Heart-of-Hearts* (my heart, soul, and psyche) for use in future *Frisuals*.

I followed these same positive-energy-producing *Steps* until I no longer had to shop in the "husky" departments but instead could finally, to my delight, fit into the jeans that I had always coveted. I'll never forget how absolutely elated I felt when I stared for minutes in front of the mirror as I fit into and bought that first pair of white jeans! What an awesome energy charge! And I made sure that once again, I stored this amazing feeling in my *Heart-of-Hearts*.

As I became a better and better athlete and my dad looked forward to spending his weekends and spare time playing paddleball and paddle tennis with me, or just watching me play and compete, I began to truly feel his love and approval, and our camaraderie led to an even stronger bond. My powerful feelings of rejection and deep sadness began to be replaced with high-voltage feelings of love, lovability, likeability, and higher self-esteem. All of this led to my developing the empowering feelings of core confidence.

As these changes took place, I would make sure that all of my *Frisuals* received the huge jolt of potent energy charges triggered by the crystal-clear realization that I truly loved the direction in which my new life was heading; that through effective *Frisualization*, I indeed had the incredible *power* to create and realize my *Gold* and *Truth*; and that I could keep on attaining all these great, empowering things by continuing to make *Golden* and *Truthful* life choices.

Through my proactive efforts to update and keep my *Gold* and *Truth*, and therefore my *Frisuals*, current, I continued to tap into *the* most potent combination of energy charges available, which enabled me to become slim at the age of twelve. I've been thin ever since!

All of this was accomplished through identifying and channeling, and thereby beneficially mastering, the high-voltage, emotion-generated, toxic energy charges that in the past had overpowered me and my best judgment and led me to consistently make self-sabotaging and self-esteem-diminishing, eating-related life choices.

So what can be distilled and gleaned from this story?

1. *Your Gold* and *Your Truth* (*Your PETS*) trigger your most potent, motivating energy charges;

2. By knowing what your most precious *Gold* is and prioritizing it so that it remains at the top of your *Gold List*, you also identify what your most powerful energy charges are, for your most precious *Gold* equals your most powerful energy charges. This also applies to *Your Truth*.

    What this, in turn, enables you to do through *Frisualization* (*Frame* plus *visualization*) is to overpower and thereby negate the less potent (less motivating) energies generated from the emotions that could otherwise cloud and/or derail your intellect and your best judgment when you are faced with making important life choices at *Crunch Time!*; and

3. One of your primary goals is to *load up* each *Frisual* with *your* most powerful energy charges (your very strongest motivators), so that it is as easy and clear as possible for you to consistently make *Golden* and *Truthful* choices. (This process will be discussed in greater detail in *Step 4A*.)

Remember, you have one clear mandate and agenda whenever you construct a *Frame* or vividly *visualize* the results and consequences of your life choices: *to make a life choice that is totally consistent and in harmony with what you know* Your Gold *and* Truth *to be.*

Please note that as we discussed earlier, your *Frames* and *visuals* are carefully crafted and designed to enable *you* to push your most highly charged emotion buttons and thereby motivate yourself to make *Golden* and *Truthful* life choices.

Some In-Depth Study of the *Frisual*

In order to more fully discuss the big-picture process of developing your *Frame(s)* and *visual(s)*, let's study the following illustration:

1. You are going to attend a Christmas party tonight, and you *anticipate* that you will on a number of occasions be offered alcohol. And you *know* that you have a drinking problem that needs to be addressed and remedied.

2. You identify *Your Gold*—that is, you want to stop drinking and not risk getting another DUI; you don't want to lose your license permanently; and/or you don't want to injure or kill someone. Additionally, you want to be in control of your life and take better care of your physical, mental, and emotional well-being.

3. You acknowledge and fully appreciate that in the past, when you were offered alcohol at *Crunch Time!*, you were bombarded and overcome by emotions and their highly potent energy charges, which dismantled your thought processes and best judgment. As a result, even though in toxic-emotion-free moments you *knew* better, you

drank—to excess. Somehow, your ability to think clearly and do what you know is right for you was (figuratively and literally) drowned out at *Crunch Time!*, much like heavy static drowns out what's playing on your radio. As a result, you rationalized that:

"I *love* the easy, uninhibited feeling that I have when I'm buzzed. I'm far more social, fun, and funny, and I'm not so intense and uptight. Girls/guys like my company so much more when I'm (buzzed and) funny. Also, I *really* like the person I am when I'm buzzed better than the one when I'm not!"

This highly flawed life-choice-making left you driving home drunk, yet again!

4. Through your *Prevent Offense Steps*, with crystal clarity and rock-solid resolve, you identify the life choice that you *know* reflects *Your Gold* and *Truth*. At *Crunch Time!*, your choice will ABSOLUTELY! be, "NO ALCOHOL, FOR ANY REASON!, no matter how good it makes me feel or how attractive to girls/guys it may make me!"

5. Let's *Frame!*: "Do I want to keep drinking and risk getting another HORRIFIC! DUI? Knowing that if I keep drinking (the key here is first to load up your *Frame* with your most potent, negative *PETS*), I would risk:

   a. LOSING MY LICENSE PERMANENTLY!;

   b. experiencing even more SHAME, as I will NO LONGER BE ALLOWED TO DRIVE ANY-WHERE;

   c. having to deal with the ABHORRENT thought of how dreadfully inconvenient it would be to LOSE MY LICENSE;

d. INJURING or KILLING MY CHILDREN,
   MYSELF, and/or OTHERS!, by my driving drunk—
   which would be spiritually, emotionally, and psychologically DEVASTATING to me!;

e. suffering through LOSING CONTROL of what I
   say, how I think, and how I act when I'm drunk;

f. getting such HIDEOUS alcohol-related ILLNESSES
   AS SCLEROSIS OF THE LIVER;

g. LOSING (yet again) SOMEONE whom I LOVE
   because I'm intoxicated too much of the time;

h. being a HORRIBLE ROLE MODEL as well as an
   INATTENTIVE and IRRESPONSIBLE SINGLE
   MOTHER/FATHER to my three children; and

i. LOSING CUSTODY OF MY CHILDREN?!

All DREADFUL CONSEQUENCES of my continuing to drink!"

Then *Frame* again with the positive things that would
enhance your life if you stopped drinking. (Identify your
most potent, super-charged, positive *PETS*.) For example,
"If I say, 'NO!' to drinking and simply don't drink any longer, I will:

a. KEEP MY CHILDREN!;

b. be a much more RESPONSIBLE MOTHER/
   FATHER and a FAR BETTER ROLE MODEL;

c. KEEP CONTROL OF MY LIFE, my actions, my
   mental acuity;

d. NOT INJURE OR KILL ANYONE!, and thereby
   ruin their lives, my life, and the lives of my children;

e. KEEP MY DRIVER'S LICENSE and my mobility;

f. KEEP MEN/WOMEN IN MY LIFE with whom I want to have a relationship, with the goal that one day, I can find a good guy/girl and re-marry. I will become worthy of keeping someone good in my life and having him/her love and respect me!;

g. KEEP MY GOOD HEALTH INTACT;

h. DEVELOP THE GREAT FEELINGS OF HIGH SELF-ESTEEM AND SELF-WORTH that come along with SEIZING POSITIVE CONTROL OF MY LIFE, and feeling good about who I am and the ownership that I've taken of the things in my life that dearly count!"

6. Prioritize *Your Gold* by first thinking about THE most feared, horrific, abhorrent, shameful, guilt-inducing *consequences* that would take place should you continue to drink, followed by considering the positive gifts of your refraining from drinking. Then *visualize* them. For example, vividly *visualize*:

a. your killing your children in a car accident when you drive drunk;

b. your killing others as a result of your driving drunk;

c. your losing custody of your children because you're deemed to be an "unfit" mother;

d. your being the cause of your children feeling unloved, unwanted, and unvalued, as well as the life-long, deep-seated problems that they will develop and must suffer with;

e. your developing sclerosis of the liver or throat and/or

esophageal cancer and putting yourself at risk to suffer an early death, thereby leaving your children with no one to love and take care of them.

Your goal here is to *Frame* and *visualize* these *absolutely horrible* consequences so that they scare, appall, and sicken you to such an extent that the energy charges generated by these thoughts and *visuals* blow away and negate any other energy charges from other *less compelling* (lower-voltage) emotions, such as the need for you to satisfy your need/urge to drink.

Then do the same thing with the highly beneficial things that you would bring into your life by saying "No!" to alcohol. Once again, make sure that you *visualize* THE most WONDERFUL positives, because this *Gold* and *Truth* will be some of your most potent and generate your very highest-voltage, emotion-generated energy charges. For example, *visualize*:

a. being a great role model for your children!;

b. being there in every meaningful way for your children—who very much need and rely on you!;

c. being healthy and in control of your life!;

d. not injuring or killing anyone while driving!;

e. being able to keep people you love in your life;

f. keeping custody of your children!;

When you *Frisual*, your goal is to load up your *Frames* and *visuals* so that they are so highly emotionally charged as to enable you to make life choices that (1) reflect your clear, well thought-out, best judgment and (2) are consistent with and reflect your most dearly held *Gold* and *Truth*. The means by which you accomplish this is by channeling the energy charges of your strongest *PETS* or motivators into your *Frames* and *visuals*.

Let's now examine a story that will help explain how best to *Frisual*:

Remember "Brandon," who was ruining his life by losing wives and love-interests because of his urge/need to have sex to pornography? After speaking with him, I learned that basically he was a good, moral person, but that he had a highly poisonous psychological/behavioral problem in connection with his lovemaking. Brandon confided that he truly felt "bad" and "dirty" after the fact or act, but he couldn't seem to overpower the compulsion that always overtook him once he became intimate with his partner. He clearly knew that what he was doing was sabotaging his relationships. He said that he absolutely wanted to change his sexual behavior and become the healthy, good human being that he felt he could be, and indeed was, in many other areas of his life. He just couldn't break free of the impulse that flooded him as his relationships with his love-interests progressed.

I asked Brandon to visualize all of the great women whom he had alienated with his behavior. As he did this, I could see that this was a tremendously painful and shameful task for him. I then asked him to identify the *one* woman who *most* hurts him to think about having lost. In a flash, he said, "Kelly." He continued, with tremendous conviction, "She was the very best woman—other than my mother—who ever came into my life. She was wonderful! It absolutely kills me that I scared her away. If I ever had the chance to get her back, I'd give or do *anything*! It makes me sick. *I* make me sick!"

O.K. We now had one piece of Brandon's most potent *Gold*: Kelly—either getting her back or modifying his behavior so that if and when the next "Kelly" comes along, he won't push her away with his self-sabotaging sexual/psychological behavior.

After further discussions, I discovered two even more potent, energy-charged pieces of Brandon's *Gold*: *Brandon's deep love of his mother and the strong relationship he had with her*. Brandon truly believed that his now deceased mother was watching over him, and that she would be ashamed of his "demented" sexual behavior; and he fervently wanted his mother to be proud of him. But even more powerful was *his desire to be with his mother in heaven; and his biggest fear was that his bad behavior would preclude him from ever meeting up with her again.* This scared him to his core.

O.K. With these incredibly pure and powerful *PETS* identified, harnessed, and ready to be channeled into a *Frisual*, Brandon and I constructed the following highly loaded, and thereby amped-up, *Frame*, which he would thereafter consistently use:

1. "Do I want to continue to act in this WEAK, DIRTY, DEMENTED WAY and RISK NEVER! BEING WITH MY MOM IN HEAVEN?"; and

2. "Do I want to make MY MOM feel ASHAMED OF ME and the person I've become? Do I want her to feel the PROFOUND PAIN that I'm going through as a result of THE EMPTY/EXPLOITATIVE LIFE I'M LIVING?";

OR . . .

3. "Am I going to put an END to THIS HORRIBLE, SICKENING, SELFISH, SELF-SABOTAGING BEHAVIOR RIGHT NOW! and get back on a far better and more positive path?"

Brandon then continued to push every emotionally charged button that he could with this high-voltage resolution:

"NO MORE PORN! I WANT TO BE WITH MY MOM IN HEAVEN! I want her to be PROUD OF ME!, and I DON'T WANT TO CAUSE HER PAIN! And, I WANT KELLY BACK!"

Brandon then *visualized* the terrible consequences that he would suffer should he continue his self-sabotaging behavior. He pictured:

1. never being with his mom again (by far his most potent Gold);

2. making his mom ashamed of him;

3. causing his mom great pain;

4. losing Kelly, forever; and

5. how it would be and feel to never have a "Kelly" in his life again because of his self-sabotaging sexual behavior.

From that day on, Brandon was armed with his all-powerful *Frisual* and his pre-determined *Golden* and *Truthful* life choice that he would no longer ruin his relationships by inappropriately insisting that he be intimate or have sex to pornography. This was a clear case of *specific* anticipation by Brandon, with *Frames* and *visuals* that were locked and loaded with his most potent *PETS*.

Approximately three years later, Brandon let me know that his life and his self-image had changed "so very much for the better." Brandon said that he is in a "great and healthy" relationship with "Michelle," and that he is now free to be much more "honest," intimate, and in-the-moment with his partner, as he is no longer "a slave to that horrible behavior." He repeated that he "very rarely" watches porn anymore. But when he does, it is a joint decision, and Michelle gets turned on, too. The very positive difference, Brandon explained, is that he now feels he is no longer "selfishly exploiting" his love-interests, as he had before, because it is not all about satisfying *his* uncontrollable, urge-triggered "selfish needs."

This positive state of affairs has made Brandon feel like he is becoming a person worthy of reuniting with his mom when he passes. He also confided that when he *Frisuals* now, he substitutes Michelle as his (second) most potent *Gold*, in lieu of Kelly, who had been the love of his life—an additional, very positive and empowering outcome!

Your *Take-Aways:*

1. *Step 3* calls for you to craft your most compelling, motivating, energy-rich *Frame(s)* and *visuals(s)* in anticipation of making some future *Golden* and/or *Truthful* life choice.

2. The *Frisual*™ is a strategic formula and vehicle specifically designed to enable and empower you to consistently make *Golden* and *Truthful* life choices. It is comprised of a *Frame*™ or *Frames*™, and one or more *visuals*.

3. When you *Frame* the issue(s) before you, you stack the choice-making deck and load it with so much energy—by infusing it with so many high-voltage energy charges—that the energy charges from your potentially poisonous emotions will be overpowered and thereby nullified. As a result, you will be relatively poisonous-emotion-free at *Crunch Time!*, and thus able to think and value clearly and make life choices that are consistent with your most valued *Gold* and *Truth*.

STEP 4

Adjust the Voltage of the Energy Charges That You Will Channel into Your *Frisual(s)*

Amp Up the Energy Charges That Will Lead You to Make a *Golden* and *Truthful* Choice at *Crunch Time!*

I n constructing your most energy-charged, and therefore your most compelling, *Frames* and *visuals*, always keep this thought in mind:

> The greater the power of the energy charges that you can tap into, harness, and channel into your *Frisual*, the easier it will be for you to overpower and thereby nullify the potentially poisonous emotions that can cloud your best judgment. As a result, you are able and empowered to reason and evaluate clearly at *Crunch Time!* and are inevitably led to make a *Golden/Truthful* life choice.

Therefore, it behooves you to pile on or bundle as much heavy-duty wattage as possible into your *Frame(s)* and *visual(s)*. The means by which you can amp up your *Frisual* to the optimum is to combine the energy charges of your *PETS*, which are your truest, purest *Gold* and *Truth* (your personal motivators).

To illustrate *Step 4A*, let's discuss the case of "Rebeccah" and how she amped up the positive energy charges of her *Frame* by piling on her most potent pieces of *Gold* and *Truth*. I have entitled this story, "*So* Very Wrong, for *So* Interminably Long!":

Rebeccah got married at the age of eighteen to a very charming, wealthy, twenty-one-year-old boy named "Brent." Within months, Rebeccah was pregnant with the first of their five children and left the workforce upon learning of that first pregnancy. Financially, this was no problem for the couple, as Brent was already on the way up in his father's very successful manufacturing business. During the next twenty-two years, Rebeccah devoted herself to being the world's most loving and devoted mother and wife. However, as time passed, Brent became much less attentive to Rebeccah and more and more demeaning and abusive. One night, after coming home drunk, he became violent and pushed Rebeccah against a wall—knocking her head against it. He thereafter threatened her so that she wouldn't tell anyone about his violent behavior. To add devastating insult to injury, soon thereafter, Rebeccah heard from a friend that Brent was cheating on her with at least one of the women in his dad's company. Apparently Rebeccah and Brent hadn't made love for years, and during this time, he did everything possible to make her feel unattractive and undesirable, not to mention making her feel like a failure as both a wife and a woman.

By the time I spoke with Rebeccah, she was a shell of her former self and seemed lost. Even so, her intellect, radiant inner and outer beauty, great warmth, and sense of humor were still evident. What was also abundantly clear, however, were the profound feelings of sadness, resignation, and frustration that permeated her heart and soul. She also harbored tremendous *fear* about leaving Brent, even though she knew on many levels that he was "pure poison" for her. Essentially, she was *frozen by fear*.

When I asked Rebeccah why she hadn't left Brent years ago, she said that she had thought about it "millions of times," but that she was "too scared" to venture out on her own. For one thing, she hadn't worked for over twenty-two years, and she wouldn't know where to start. The sadness in Rebeccah's eyes reflected a woman whose beautiful spirit and love of life had been broken by Brent's abusive and manipulative behavior. Rebeccah had lost all sense and realistic perception of her abilities, talents, and blessings. As a result, she vehemently resisted making any change for the infinitely better, as she feared she couldn't survive away from the poisonous and painful life she had with Brent.

As Rebeccah and I began to work together, our initial goal was to free her of her crippling fear so that she would be able to see, reason, make choices, and act with *Golden/Truthful* clarity. Over the next few weeks, we began to identify Rebeccah's *PETS* (her *Gold* and *Truth*) and incorporated them into a *List* of her aspirations:

1. to neither cause nor in any way encourage her daughters to feel that Rebeccah's toxic, abusive, and demeaning marriage to Brent is the kind of relationship that they should seek out or allow themselves to be in; nor did she want to cause or in any way encourage her sons to believe that emulating Brent's sick behavior would ever be acceptable (and therefore, she had to become a healthier, stronger, and better role model for her children);

2. to "find" herself again; to regain her inner strength, confidence, spirit, self-esteem, and clarity; and to once again "like" and "love" who she is;

3. to be self-supportive so that she would never be beholden to or dependent upon Brent—or any man—ever again; and

4. to establish a loving, healthy, strong, and stable home for her children, who are still in school and living with her.

As I continued to counsel Rebeccah, she dug deeper and deeper into her mind, heart, soul, and psyche. As a result, she was able to mine many more highly potent nuggets of *Gold* and *Truth* (her very strongest motivators and emotional triggers) and bundle and infuse them into her *Frame* and *visuals*, thereby significantly amping up her positive energy charges. Here's Rebeccah's super-potent *Frame* that decimated the once supremely potent energy charges generated by her deep-seated fear of leaving Brent and their marriage:

"Do I want to leave Brent and my marriage and:

1. be a POSITIVE, HEALTHY, STRONG ROLE MODEL FOR MY CHILDREN and not expose them for one minute more to my HOR-RIBLY TOXIC, ABUSIVE, DEMEANING RELATIONSHIP with Brent;

2. be my BEST SELF again and thereby regain my CONFIDENCE; the LOVE and good feelings in my heart and soul; my OPTIMISM; and my SELF-ESTEEM;

3. be RID OF the constant FEAR, POISON, SICKNESS, HURT, PAIN, AND DEGRADATION that I've been subjected to all these years;

4. one day be in a HEALTHY, LOVING, POSITIVE, RESPECTFUL, CHERISHING RELATIONSHIP with a great, warm, loving, support-ive man; and

5. physically, psychologically, and emotionally feel, once again, like the 'me' I so long to be?;

OR . . .

Do I want to again succumb to and be frozen by my intense fears and (thereby) remain trapped in a SICK, DEBILITATING, POISONOUS, PAINFUL EXISTENCE and continue to:

1. CAUSE or encourage my DAUGHTERS TO DATE and marry HORRIFIC MEN like Brent;

2. encourage or allow my son to believe that emulating Brent is in any way O.K. or acceptable;

3. be a DEPLORABLE ROLE MODEL for my children;

4. HATE! who I've become;

5. HATE! my weakness;

6. be ASHAMED! of who I am;

7. HATE! that I've WASTED all my valuable time with someone who is ABUSIVE;

8. HATE! how he treats me; and

9. HATE! that my fears have stopped me from doing what I've known for years is the healthy thing for me to do? . . . that is, to leave Brent as fast as I can?!"

By Rebeccah piling on *so many* high-voltage *PETS*, thereby amping up her collective motivating energy charges to a supremely potent level, Rebeccah rendered the energy charges generated by her fears virtually powerless. As a result, when she *Framed* the issue as she did, her inevitable answer was: "I NEVER! want to be in a HORRIBLY POISONOUS RELATIONSHIP ever again! I don't want to be with him [Brent] another minute! I'm just sorry I've wasted so much time and subjected us all to such TOXIC BEHAVIOR. I'M SO READY! to do, be, and feel much better!"

Within weeks thereafter, Rebeccah left Brent, and a few days later, she filed for divorce.

Today, a few years later, Rebeccah's inner light burns brightly and radiates for all who know her to see. She is well on her way to being the mother, woman, role model, professional, and overall happier person whom she envisioned when she first compiled her *Gold* and *Truth Lists*, and thereafter made and acted upon her decision to leave Brent.

What's important to glean here is that one of the primary reasons why Rebeccah's *Frisual* led her to make such a clear, easy, and inevitable choice to shed her fears and immediately leave Brent was that she so very effectively piled on, and thereby amped up, her *Golden* and *Truthful* energy charges. As a result, the once strong, but now significantly weakened, energy charges that were triggered by her deep-seated fears about leaving Brent were decisively overpowered and thereby nullified.

Your *Take-Away*:

In order to ensure that the energy charges in your *Frames* and *visuals* are *the* very strongest, and therefore the most effective, possible, it is essential that you pile on or bundle as many of your high-voltage pieces of *Gold* and *Truth* as you can and then channel them into your *Frames* and *visuals*.

Dissipate the Potency of the Energy Charges That Can/Will Lead You to Make Self-Destructive and/or Self-Sabotaging Choices at *Crunch Time!*

S*tep 4B* is devoted to your dissipating the highly potent energy charges generated by potentially poisonous emotions; as a result, your goal is to significantly weaken or negate the potentially poisonous energy charges that can motivate you to make a self-defeating or a self-sabotaging life choice.

Before we move forward, let's take a moment to define the term *Destructive, Emotion-Triggered Scripting*, as we will refer to it in many instances throughout the rest of our journey. As we have discussed, certain individuals, events, and things evoke highly potent emotion-, impulse-, or urge-generated energy charges within you. These energy charges in turn trigger what we will call *Destructive, Emotion-Generated Scripting*, or those behavioral scripts or patterns of behavior that are physically, psychologically, emotionally, and/or spiritually destructive to you and/or others. Often, these toxic scripts are so deeply embedded within your psyche that they have become reflexive, as you automatically act them out time and again.

In *Step 4B*, we have two objectives:

1. to significantly dissipate the potent energy charges triggered by your potentially destructive emotions so that when you *Frisual*, you think and reason with clarity and precision, and thereby make a *Golden/Truthful* life choice; and

2. to break up and put a *definitive end* to any and all *Destructive, Emotion-Triggered Scripting* that you have.

As you are beginning to see, *Your Killer Emotions* is in many ways focused on significantly *increasing* the power of the energy charges that will motivate and lead you to make *Golden/Truthful* life choices. It also calls for you to materially *decrease* the potency of the energy charges that have in the past led, and still have the strong potential to lead, you to make self-defeating and self-sabotaging choices in the future. In *Step 4A*, we discussed how to *amp up* your potentially positive energy charges. Now, in *Step 4B*, we will focus on how to *significantly decrease* the voltage of your potentially poisonous energy charges through the process of *Toxic-Energy-Charge Dissipation*™ or *TECD*™.

By way of analogy, let me explain the process of *Toxic-Energy-Charge Dissipation*. The other day, I was admiring how my very wise and kind executive assistant, Shari Freis, was on the phone attentively and compassionately listening to a client unload all of her professionally related frustration and unhappiness with her employer. After about forty-five minutes of venting, the client calmed down and thereafter thanked Shari for being such a gracious and supportive sounding board.

After that call, I asked Shari why she spends so much of her very valuable time listening as she did. She responded, "Because, if the client purges with me, they run out of steam, and their frustration and anger levels significantly lessen. So when they later talk to you, they're much more relaxed, as well as far more focused on and *clear* about what they really need to accomplish."

"You are *truly* brilliant, Shari," I told her.

This form of purging or venting is very similar to the process of *Toxic-Energy-Charge Dissipation*. The purging allows the clients to *dissipate* or get rid of the angst, anger, frustration, fear, and/or "steam" that they have bottled up and have allowed to flood them. Afterward, in a cool, calm, and intelligent manner, they are then able to focus on and deal with the true issue at hand. Similarly, the process of *Toxic-Energy-Charge Dissipation* enables you to significantly diminish the intensity of your most powerful negative energy charges; as a result, when you *Frisual*, your positive energy charges can more easily override, and thereby nullify, your now significantly weakened negative ones. Thus, you are free to think clearly, exercise your best judgment, and make *Golden/Truthful* life choices at *Crunch Time!*.

There are many levels of strength and depth (depending upon a number of variables) of the toxic, emotion-generated energy charges that you will want to effectively dissipate before you *Frisual*. For simplicity, we will divide the potency of these charges into two categories:

1. *Regular-strength*, potentially toxic energy charges. In many instances you, working alone, can effectively lessen the potency of these charges; and

2. Long-term and/or deeply embedded *extra-strength*, potentially toxic energy charges. In dealing with these deep-seated, emotion-triggered challenges and mastering their high-voltage energy charges, along with following *Step 4B*, it is possible that you will need to seek the aid of a qualified therapist or counselor.[9]

---

9 At the end of this book, please see: *Some Suggestions for Your Therapist or Counselor Regarding* Extra-Strength, Toxic-Energy-Charge Dissipation™ (TECD™) *and Destructive, Generational, Emotion-Triggered Scripting.*

In connection with your *Prevent Offense*, please keep the following in mind:

1. First and foremost, ideally you will prepare your *Prevent Offense* weeks or months *before* you are called upon to make an important life choice. As a result, you may well have the necessary time to work through *Step 4B* by yourself, or when necessary, with a therapist or counselor;

2. The extremely high-voltage, toxic energy charges that you will endeavor to dissipate often come from deeply entrenched emotions and/or long-term scripting; as a result, some time-consuming self-exploration will be necessary in order for you to identify, understand, and fully appreciate where these poisonous energy charges come from and how they have adversely affected you. Ideally, *The Prevent Offense* contemplates giving you the time you'll need to effectively engage in this self-exploration process; and

3. It is assumed that when you prepare your *Prevent Offense*, you are making a clear, non-emotion-clouded choice to put an end to being dismantled by your poisonous emotion-generated energy charges at *Crunch Time!*, and that you are not in a toxic-emotion-flooded state while you are going through the *Prevent Offense* process. Therefore, with great clarity and pinpoint precision, you can prepare yourself to make *Golden* and *Truthful* life choices at *Crunch Time!*.

Let's now discuss why *Toxic-Energy-Charge Dissipation (TECD)* is so important to you. As we discussed earlier, one of the essential differences between the dog that salivated when it heard a bell ring in Pavlov's stimulus-response experiment and a human being is that a human being is able to consciously and carefully think, evaluate, and reason after a stimulus is presented and *before choosing* to act or to refrain from acting. Therefore, we are able to consciously make *value-based* choices. *However*, when we are presented with a stimulus (a certain person, event, thing, or thought) that strikes a deep chord in our psyche, we often automatically and unthinkingly act out a destructive script of behavior. These *Destructive, Emotion-Triggered Scripts* are our means of navigating through the murky—and often torrential—waters of life. Many of our scripts are designed to protect us from being emotionally, psychologically, and/or physically hurt (again!). They are our real-life adaptations. The key concepts here are as follows:

Supremely high-voltage, toxic energy charges triggered by certain people, events, things, and perceptions often result in us reflexively (and therefore, unthinkingly) and repeatedly acting out our destructive, self-sabotaging scripts of behavior to our great detriment. In most instances, acting out these destructive scripts is completely at odds with what we truly want in and for the long term of our lives (our *Gold*) and who we ideally would like to be (our *Truth*). And, as we continually make poor, destructive, and self-sabotaging life choices, we lose valuable, empowering self-esteem and our all-important inner core confidence to believe that we can truly accomplish our cherished life goals and dreams, and be the person who we aspire to be. Therefore, when this highly toxic, emotion-triggered scripting is combined with extremely low levels of self-esteem and exceedingly strong feelings of hopelessness deep-seated within your *Heart-of-Hearts* (your heart, mind, and psyche), you will be far more likely to continue to act out the same destructive script in every instance in which you're presented with certain stimuli.

As an illustration of this dynamic, let's examine the case of "Leslie":

Leslie is an actress who had a highly lucrative and prestigious regular role on a popular network daytime "soap." What I have learned about

Leslie is that there is something in her background that makes her perceive and feel that everyone is out to "shaft" her. And when Leslie perceives and feels that certain actions taken by others toward her are disrespectful or, as she puts it, "just plain wrong!" extremely strong and highly toxic energy charges are triggered within her. The predictable result of this is that Leslie *consistently* acts out the same self-sabotaging script of flying into a blinding rage and *unthinkingly* reacting in a highly self-destructive and self-sabotaging manner.

This is exactly what happened when Leslie perceived and felt that her management's offer for a new series contract was a "disgrace" and a clear effort to "shaft" her. She felt this way despite the fact that her management offered her a token raise during the economically challenging latter half of 2008. Apparently, as soon as Leslie heard management's initial offer, all of her pent-up feelings of pain, hurt, and rejection were triggered and began to bubble over. These heightened, ugly feelings in turn triggered tremendously potent energy charges within her, which led her to make the self-destructive choice to lash out and retaliate against her management by:

1. telling her management that if they didn't give her the kind of raise "she deserves," she wouldn't report to work at the end of the month when her contract expired; and

2. signing a long-term contract with a talent representative with an unsavory reputation, whom she knew her management hated dealing with, simply in order "to spite" her management.

The catastrophic result was that Leslie's management withdrew their offer to her and immediately removed her from the show. When the emotional dust settled, and both intellectual clarity and the stark reality set in that she had lost her job and had no other job to go to, Leslie panicked. Her best judgment told her that "she screwed up . . . in a BIG way!" Initially, she directed her new representative to go back to her management and request that they reinstate their offer and her job. However, her management was only too happy to tell this (loathed) representative, "No! It's too late. She (Leslie) should have thought about the repercussions of her acts and threats *before* she drew her line in the sand."

Upon receiving this horrible news, Leslie became even more terrified. She then personally went to management (with her tail between her legs) and basically begged for her job back—*even if she received no raise*. Unfortunately for Leslie, management had lived through "way too many" of her angry reactions. They told Leslie's representative that they were "over her," as "Life's just too short!" As a result, Leslie was informed that she should pack up her things and "be off the lot by the end of the day."

Devastated in every way, Leslie left her job with no other position to go to and with no prospects of future employment during a terrible economic time. Additionally, she was under a long-term contract to a talent representative whom she would quickly grow to disrespect, dislike, and be embarrassed by. This all transpired because certain deep-seated emotions and highly potent energy charges were triggered within Leslie, fueling her to *unthinkingly* react and lash out in a most self-sabotaging manner . . . , which was consistent with how she had acted *countless* times before!

O.K. Let's move on to *your* scripting. Please know that breaking up (with) deeply embedded *Destructive, Emotion-Triggered Scripting is* hard to do! . . . but, it can indeed be done! In this *Step*, we're going to examine how to accomplish it.

For our study, we will focus on the two primary places from which our scripts originate:

1. our genes; and

2. our environmental adaptations.

In connection with genetics, I would like to share the following insight with you, which was formulated and written by my mom, Betty Lindner, for her documentary about my dad, "There Goes My Heart: The Jack Lindner Story": "Some or many of our feelings, thoughts, behaviors, inclinations, and scripts are encoded in our (and our ancestors') DNA. Therefore, we inherit these traits through our genes." Below is an excerpt from the documentary regarding this process:

> *Believe it or not, there is an incredibly important "open secret" that most of us pay little or no attention to. I'm referring to a series of essential facts that affect each and every life to a considerable degree.*
>
> *Metaphorically, life is a special kind of "scripted dream." A dream in very High Definition. Our individual dreams are initiated when we are conceived; when sperm fertilizes the egg; and when the very first cell divides. Wondrously, it is then—from the highly complicated processes of combining, deleting, and recombining of DNA, RNA, genes, proteins, and the necessary chemistry—that, depending in part upon which genes are activated and which genes remain dormant along the way, our initial "personal scripts" originate, and continue to develop with each cell division.*
>
> *It should be noted that the "positives" (e.g., a Mozart's musical gifts) along with the "negatives" (e.g., "the sins of the fathers" and no less those "of the mothers") are all incorporated into the genes of offspring during this process. However, it is only when specific genes are activated and expressed in the then current scripts of their children that the "gifts" and "sins" of the parents are actually visited upon their children, who then continue the process when they subsequently procreate.*

Hence, our genes are "hand-me-downs" and "carry-overs" inherited from our early forbears and direct ancestors. Thus we are never tabula rasa (a blank slate). We are, in a manner of speaking, "time travelers" and "transporters" of our personal histories (thoughts, feelings, behaviors, and scripts) from eons of yesterdays, to millions of nows, which were once millions of tomorrows.

Our scripts are also determined by what we learn and experience throughout our lives. Therefore, both heredity (our genetic endowment) and environment play major roles in our scripting.

I agree with my mom's very astute belief that some of our scripts of behavior are inherited from our ancestors, as they are encoded in our DNA and have been passed on from generation to generation.[10]

The second primary means by which we derive our scripts is through life experience or learned behaviors that we develop in order to help us get through life. Ironically, these coping mechanisms that we develop in order to protect us from (further) emotional, psychological, and/or physical pain are often the same defensive scripts that can lead us to take our most destructive and self-sabotaging actions.

For our study, let's view how we develop our personal (non-genetic) scripts of behavior—or coping mechanisms—with the following explanation of your *Heart-of-Hearts* that appears in my book, *Crunch Time!: The 8 Steps to Making the Right Life Decisions at the Right Times*:[11, D]

It's arguable that all of us have a profound need to be loved and treasured, a need that we experience in the

---

10 But regardless of whether my mother and I are correct or not, this theory has absolutely no bearing on the efficacy of *The 7 Steps*.

11 Whereas *Your Killer Emotions* focuses on your emotions and how they impact your life choices, *Crunch Time* is devoted to the cognitive component of decision-making.

deepest recesses of our being. This need, as I understand it, is two-pronged: Not only must we in fact be loved, treasured, and respected, but we must also feel loved, cherished, and respected by our parents, key caregivers, and significant others. Since children aren't mind readers, the love and treasuring given to them must be communicated in ways that children can recognize, understand, and experience from the moment of birth (e.g., initially through touch, sound, and warmth) onward. So even if parents have the best of intentions, if they can't effectively communicate their love to their children in a way that their children can understand or initially feel, it's all for naught. As time goes on, children will subjectively interpret the stimuli that they take in (e.g., how parents and significant others act toward them) as a means of determining how these individuals feel about them and ultimately how these children perceive and feel about themselves.

Looking at the big picture of my development, it's clear that whether or not I felt and perceived that my needs were met in a given situation determined my feelings about certain situations or individuals, and whether or not I made constructive or destructive choices regarding them thereafter.

How children's needs are met and how children subjectively perceive and feel that they are regarded have a major and lasting impact upon them; ultimately, these perceptions and feelings determine what scripts they will adopt and act out during the course of their lives. This concept can most easily be explained through imagination and visualization.

First, create and visualize in your mind a highly

simplified metaphorical version of a child's heart. In the depths of this metaphorical heart is a magic place. (This is similar to the metaphorical and/or metaphysical concept of the "seat" of your soul or the core of your being and acts, much like the mind as it functions and relates to the brain.) I refer to this metaphorical, magical place as the Heart-of-Hearts.

Except for a small, but strong, metaphorical 'magnet' within that represents the child's fundamental and primal needs, the Heart-of-Hearts appears relatively empty at birth. The primary function of this magnet is to attract and draw in emotional stimuli from the outer world.

These stimuli are then recognized and received either as nurturing and enhancing, or as diminishing and hurtful. Thus, from the very beginning of the child's life, the child's Heart-of-Hearts is gradually filled with whatever is experienced and drawn in from the child's outer world.

Now, think back and try to remember and visualize what it was like to be an innocent child—completely open and trusting, with a need for love, approval, and acceptance in order to flourish psychologically, while at the same time being just as completely open, trusting, vulnerable, and wholly defenseless against rejection, hurt, pain, and disappointment—all at the hands of parents and/or the significant impactful others you were totally dependent upon or exposed to during your childhood years. The subsequent influence of all of this on 'you' (your Heart-of-Hearts) was most profound. It touched and impacted the very core of your being—for better or worse—depending on how you perceived the experiences. In this regard, you must stay fully aware that because all children and adults are exposed to various different stimuli, they each perceive and process them in their own subjective ways.

Next, imagine that the Heart-of-Hearts *is magical because it has the power, in certain instances, to process one form of energy into another—such as when the gases of hydrogen and oxygen are transformed into water; when water is boiled and transformed into steam; or when water is frozen and transformed into ice.*

When the Heart-of-Hearts *draws in both the positive and negative stimuli that it receives from the outside world, it magically transforms them from sensory perceptions into various good and bad feelings that, in turn, fill it up. Thereafter, if the amount of felt love, positive valuing, and respect in the* Heart-of-Hearts *is plentiful enough to exceed a specific threshold (the near complete filling of the* Heart-of-Hearts*), then there are enough feelings of love, high self-esteem, and self-respect for some of the feelings to be transformed into other feelings: first, into self-love; then, into the love of others; and finally, into altruism.*

Feelings of being loved (lead to) → *high self-esteem and self-respect* → *self-love* → *love of others* → *altruistic love*

Optimally, a child's Heart-of-Hearts *will be filled to overflowing with feelings of love and being cherished, feelings that have been bestowed upon the child from the moment of birth by parents and/or other key individuals. Once a child's* Heart-of-Hearts *is filled with love and other positive feelings, there essentially will be no room left within the* Heart-of-Hearts *for any negative stimuli to penetrate. In essence, the child's* Heart-of-Hearts *is so well insulated and fortified psychologically, emotionally, and spiritually by positive feelings that the negativity rolls off the child like water off a duck's back. Maybe this, in part, explains why some children and adults can be exposed to negative stimuli—such as violent films, TV programs, and music—without being affected by them, whereas others are catalyzed to commit destructive acts.*

If a child's Heart-of-Hearts *is left partially or totally unfilled with positive feelings from parents and significant others, this can allow the magnet within (the child's needs) to indiscriminately attract both negative and positive stimuli that will fill the* Heart-of-Hearts*—and the big problem today is that there are so many negative stimuli in our society to attract (such as violence, crime, and poor role models, to name just a few).*

In many instances, when feelings of being loved, valued, and respected aren't initially forthcoming from parents or significant others in a child's life, and when these positive feelings are perceived by the child to be totally unavailable, *the* Heart-of-Hearts *frequently fills up and begins to overflow with overwhelming feelings of* hopelessness, unlovability, unworthiness, rejection, betrayal, inadequacy, shame, hurt, resentment, alienation, insecurity, *and* powerlessness, *depending upon what the child perceives and/or experiences.*

Along with the feelings of unlovability and hurt, there also develop a sense of extreme vulnerability and an intense fear of having that vulnerability exposed. At some point during this process, the child's hunger for love, valuing, approval, and respect is psychologically suppressed (i.e., as a defense mechanism, it is pressed back into the Heart-of-Hearts, *where it is transformed). From then on, new needs arise and* behavioral scripts are developed *to give the child perceived protection, power, control, and revenge. However, despite the fact that a large variety of rationalizations, as well as a number of other coping strategies and defense mechanisms (scripts), may have been developed and put into place, when frustration after frustration, and hurt after hurt are added to the already existing negative feelings, they are all too often transformed in the* Heart-of-Hearts *of a child or an adult into the unreasoning and powerful emotions of intense anger, rage, and hate.*

Feeling unloved (leads to) → frustration → hopelessness → pain and hurt → resentment, anger, and rage → destructive and self-sabotaging behavior

When these emotions come into play, as they are forced to in almost all love- and respect-starved cases, they can and often do result in destructive actions taken (and destructive scripts developed) by those experiencing them. These actions may be taken against oneself—like self-sabotage—and/or against others. Sometimes these actions aren't related to the behavior of the targeted person, such as in the instance of displaced anger when, for example, an employer has a negative encounter with his wife, child, or valued client and then immediately thereafter yells at or humiliates someone else, such as an employee, who played no role in the causal event.

I have also seen instances when the emotions of anger, hate, and rage can be totally out of proportion to the situations in which they are evoked. This might explain the extreme incident that I heard about when one student accidentally bumped into another student in the corridor of their high school. The student who was bumped reacted instantly by reaching into his backpack, pulling out a 9mm handgun, and shooting the student who bumped into him. Essentially, the seething anger within this person was like a keg of dynamite just looking and longing for a match and a flame. (Very much like the seething anger in Leslie, whom we discussed earlier, which was ready to come rushing to the fore as soon as she felt disrespected.)

When parents or significant others don't fill their children's Heart-of-Hearts *with enough love; and when their children fail to develop a strong sense of emotional, psychological, and physical acceptance, along with positive feelings of belonging, these children will try to find other ways to satisfy these needs. Often the satisfaction of these intense needs results in individuals making destructive and self-sabotaging choices.*

So, the basic law of one's Heart-of-Hearts *is that what goes into your* Heart-of-Hearts *comes out in one form or another. When love, respect, treasuring,* positive feelings, *and* positive perceptions *of yourself fill your* Heart-of-Hearts, *healthy and constructive feelings, choices, and behaviors result. When negative and unhealthy feelings and perceptions fill it, unhealthy and destructive feelings, choices, actions, and* Destructive, Emotion-Triggered Scripting *result.*

We all have been exposed to a unique combination of healthy and unhealthy experiences, treatments, and values, and our Heart-of-Hearts *has been filled accordingly with varying amounts of positive and negative feelings*

and perceptions. For many of us, that fortuitous combi-
nation dictates what forms our scripts will take, includ-
ing what our defense mechanisms for dealing and coping
with life's challenges are.

As a means of illustrating the workings of one's *Heart-of-Hearts*, I'd like to share the case of "Carla" with you. "Ruth," one of Carla's relatives, contacted me to see if I could ameliorate what Ruth perceived as an explainable, but totally untenable, situation. As I have not yet worked with Carla, these are my perceptions and thoughts based upon what has been told to me:

Carla is a forty-eight-year-old mother of three children, "Britt," "Greg," and "Tiffany." Britt, who is twenty-one years old, recently graduated from college; Greg, who is nineteen, is a college sophomore; and Tiffany, who had been working for an accounting firm, was laid off and is out of work. She is twenty-four. Recently, Carla's husband of seven years, "Ryan," came home one night and told Carla that he wanted a divorce. He moved out of their Phoenix-based home that evening. Carla's first husband, "Steve," had divorced her after nine years of marriage.

On the one hand, Carla was stunned. But on the other, she and Ryan had been suffering through marital discord for years. By many accounts, Carla is smart, attractive, and very talented; but she is also very rigid and exceedingly controlling in almost all aspects of her life. Ryan appears to be passive and compliant when compared to Carla.

In the eyes of their children, Carla's controlling and demeaning behavior caused the rift between their parents and made it appear as if the sweet-natured Ryan was left with no other choice than to leave the marriage. What seemed to disturb Carla most was the fact that after Ryan abandoned her, Britt, Greg, and Tiffany chose to spend most of their available time with their affable father, thereby abandoning her, as well!

After losing her job and trying for months to find a comparable position during the economically challenging year of 2008, Tiffany was still out of work and almost out of money on which to live. As a result, she asked Carla if she (Tiffany) could come back to Phoenix and live in Carla's three-bedroom home with her in order to minimize her expenses until she landed a job and could get back on her feet financially. Despite the fact that Carla lived alone in her spacious house since her separation from Ryan, Carla coldly denied her daughter's request for help. Carla's explanation for her astonishing refusal was that she wanted to "live *alone*." She said that she didn't want to spend any money on anyone (but herself), as she needed to make sure that she had enough money on which to survive for the rest of her life.

Ruth said that my goal in all of this would be to essentially help Carla "open her heart" and encourage Carla to change her mind both about allowing Tiffany to come live with her and helping Greg with his college expenses (which Carla could apparently afford to do).

At this point, it is important and may be quite elucidating to discuss certain relevant aspects of Carla's generational history. Carla's grandmother, "Greta," had a father who died when Greta was four years old. Greta was then abandoned by her mother. So Greta grew up psychologically, emotionally, and physically abandoned in an orphanage. As a direct result, Greta's *Heart-of-Hearts* was full with feelings of hurt, anger, betrayal, and unlovability. By all accounts, Greta didn't know how to love and gave no love, warmth, or compassion to her children . . . who, in turn, felt psychologically and emotionally abandoned and betrayed. One of these children was Carla's mother, "Charisse." At some point, Carla's parents, Charisse and "Carl," divorced, leaving Carla to feel abandoned and betrayed. To make matters worse, throughout her life, Carla perceived that her parents favored her brother "Alex" over her. When her parents divorced, this favoritism became even more evident. So more feelings of abandonment, betrayal, hurt, anger, and unlovability welled up within Carla's *Heart-of-Hearts*.

As mentioned previously, her husband, Ryan, left her. Then Carla began to realize that her children sided with their "victimized" dad! As a result, Carla's *Heart-of-Hearts* was now flooded with deeply embedded feelings of abandonment, betrayal, unlovability, and deep anger. It is in the context of this repeated, profound *Destructive, Generational, Emotion-Triggered Scripting* that Carla's choices not to allow her daughter, Tiffany, to live with her and her stone-cold refusal to help her son, Greg, with his expenses must be examined.

The tremendously powerful energy charges that have all but blocked and/or dismantled Carla's reasoning processes and best judgment at *Crunch Time!* appear to have in large part come from her deep-seated feelings of:

1. repeated abandonment;

2. repeated betrayal;

3. unlovability;

4. hopelessness;

5. very low self-esteem;

6. intense frustration;

7. anger; and

8. rage.

All of the high-voltage toxic energy charges from these supremely negative, self-esteem-deflating feelings filled, to overflowing, Carla's *Heart-of-Hearts*. And, as we said earlier: What goes into your *Heart-of-Hearts* in one form or another at some point comes out. So when feelings of abandonment, hopelessness, vulnerability, rejection, and unlovability go into your *Heart-of-Hearts*, behavioral scripts are developed in order to give the individual perceived protection, power, and control, which may manifest itself as revenge. As a result, Carla adopted and learned at least three self-destructive behavioral scripts in order to protect herself from being hurt/abandoned anymore:

1. seeking to control everything and everyone in her life;

2. being extremely rigid; and

3. going into physical, psychological, and emotional retreat and repression mode.

Carla used these scripts in order to enable her to feel and be less vulnerable and to protect her heart, soul, and psyche from being hurt any further. Additionally, in connection with her seemingly "unfeeling" decision to not let Tiffany live with her, Carla had taken out much of the feelings of rejection, anger, hurt, and pain that she has experienced and transferred it to Tiffany. According to Carla, she wanted to "live alone" and not give anything to Tiffany or Greg because, as she allegedly said, "At the end of the day, that's [money is] all there is, right?" Obviously, Carla's flawed thought process here is that if she dearly clings to her money, she won't lose that too, as she very painfully perceives and feels that she has lost everyone and everything else of importance in her life.

As we will soon discuss, it will be through Carla engaging in some heavy-duty *Energy-Charge Dissipation* that she should be able to significantly diminish the potency of her highly toxic energy charges; break the chains of her *Destructive, Emotion-Triggered Scripting*; and thereby begin to make love-based *Golden* and *Truthful* life choices.

The Complementary Process of Your Proactively Instilling Positive Feelings into Your *Heart-of-Hearts* When You Utilize *Toxic-Energy-Charge Dissipaters*

Let's now consider three levels of motivation and energy-charge expression:

1. The *lowest* level of energy-charge expression is performing acts out of fear, sadness, loneliness, hurt, anger, and hate. For example, when one acts out of fear, whether it's out of fear of punishment, going to "hell" or "purgatory," or getting caught, the motive for acting in such a manner isn't highly evolved.

2. The next or *middle* level is performing acts with "karma" as your motivation. That is, you perform a certain act because you *expect* or *hope* for something good to come back to you in return. And while I believe that karma in some form does exist, and acting in hopes of a karmic "payback" is more evolved than acting out of, say, "fear," such giving still can, in many instances, be "conditional."

3. The *highest* level of motivation and energy-charge expression is acting *altruistically*. Altruistic acts are acts of *love*, *forgiveness*, *appreciation*, *respect*, *gratitude*, and *empathy* that have nothing to do with an expectation of receiving some payback in kind down the road. Altruistic acts are performed purely because they are intrinsically the right things to do, with no regard for any karmic benefit that you might receive. These are acts undertaken *unconditionally*.

However, as it turns out, you *do* receive an incredibly tangible *indirect* benefit when you engage in altruistic acts of *Toxic-Energy-Charge Dissipation*, such as *loving others; forgiving, understanding,* and *respecting others;* and being *compassionate, sympathetic,* and *empathetic to others.* When you perform these acts, they not only dissipate your highly toxic energy charges, but the successful performance of these acts fills your *Heart-of-Hearts* with positive feelings about and perceptions of yourself. These feelings and perceptions in turn catalyze you to make more positive choices and take more positive actions. So one positive choice and act beget other positive ones, which continue to fill your *Heart-of-Hearts* with feelings of high self-esteem and high self-worth. And you in turn will make more and more positive life choices for yourself because you, in your *Heart-of-Hearts,* feel that you are *truly worth* making constructive and enhancing decisions for.

The more you have feelings of high self-worth, the more you develop and feel the empowering feelings of self-love. And once you feel true self-love, you are far more likely to be forgiving and understanding of others and yourself, as well as loving, respectful, and compassionate. So one process (utilizing *Toxic-Energy-Charge Dissipation*) feeds and is completely complementary to the other (instilling positive feelings and perceptions into your *Heart-of-Hearts*).

Additionally, by trying to unconditionally forgive and by endeavoring to understand, respect, appreciate, and love others and show compassion and empathy/sympathy for them, as you will soon see, you put the percentages strongly in your favor that you will more easily and effectively diffuse your toxic energy charges, as well as put an end to your *Destructive, Emotion-Triggered Scripting.*

As they say, *Namasté:* Let the love, light, and goodness in you see, appreciate, and celebrate these things in others! The results will be *Heart-of-Hearts*-nourishing for everyone involved!

Destructive, Generational, Emotion-Triggered Scripting

Earlier we discussed that our *Destructive, Emotion-Triggered Scripting* can come from two sources: our genetics and our own life adaptations. We also said that certain toxic, emotion-generated energy charges and certain *Destructive, Emotion-Triggered Scripting* are extremely difficult to dissipate and break up, respectively, because they are deeply embedded in our psyches. In a number of cases that I have encountered, three of which we will soon discuss, it seems likely that a person's *Destructive, Emotion-Triggered Scripting* and the accompanying, extremely high-voltage energy charges have been created and built up, respectively, *over several generations*. Additionally, it can be argued that the tremendous energy-charge build-up in these cases comes from these individuals' highly charged genetic endowment, which is combined with the feelings of hurt, pain, anger, abuse, rejection, and lack of respect that they have suffered during their lives.

With these challenges in mind, let's study how you can dissipate your toxic, emotion-generated energy charges through the cases of "Carla," "Cassie," and "Philip." I go into some depth to explain these individuals' backgrounds because many of the emotional problems that these individuals have are genetically related and/or rooted. Additionally, by understanding how I either would help or have already helped these individuals to handle their deep-seated emotional challenges, you will glean insights as to how you and/or your therapist or counselor can significantly diminish the potency of your deeply entrenched toxic energy charges through utilizing the *Toxic-Energy-Charge Dissipaters* of your being *understanding, forgiving, compassionate, sympathetic/empathetic,* and *loving*.

As we begin our discussions of the above-mentioned cases, please be keenly aware of how very important it is for all three of the individuals—Carla, Cassie, and Philip—to be *conscious* of, understand, and appreciate who they are, their unique histories, and where relevant others are coming from when they endeavor to make their *Golden/Truthful* life choices. This is essential, as one of the primary means of dissipating highly potent, destructive energy charges is through the *Energy-Charge Dissipater* of *understanding*:

1. *Who you are and your generational history.* That's why identifying your purest *Gold* and *Truth* is so important. As discussed earlier, what is also essential is to identify and acknowledge that you have certain self-defeating, emotion-triggered behavioral patterns or emotion-triggered scripts, which have *repeatedly* led you to make self-destructive life choices. If possible, *it is highly beneficial for you to understand from where and from whom these patterns and scripts come and how they have negatively affected you*; and

2. *Where others are coming from.* As you will glean from the upcoming cases/stories, if you can know and understand the reasons *why* relevant others act as they do and/or understand their histories, this can go a long way in dissipating the potency of the poisonous energy charges that you are dealing with regarding a life choice. Here's why: With knowledge comes understanding; and with understanding comes appreciation and/or identification, which can lead to your feeling compassion, sympathy, and/or empathy. In time, these feelings can lead to forgiveness; and once you can feel compassion and truly forgive, you can then feel love and love others.

As you will see, this evolutionary process is essential in empowering you to break the chains of the destructive scripts that bind and derail you. Here's the visual of this process:

Toxic-Energy-Charge Dissipation™/Destructive, Emotion-Triggered Scripting Negation

Love of Others

↑

Forgiveness of Others

↑

Compassion, Sympathy, and/or Empathy for Others

↑

Appreciation and/or Respect for Others

↑

Understanding of Others

↑

Knowledge of Others

A story regarding the *Toxic-Energy-Charge Dissipater* of gaining understanding of others and where they are coming from that almost always resonates with my clients and those with whom I consult is one that took place when I was very young:

One day, when I was ten years old, my friend "Gary" and I went to Manhattan to see a New York Knicks basketball game. We decided to eat at a fast-food restaurant that served big drinks, big burgers, and big baked potatoes filled with lots of tasty, gooey toppings. As we got our food and began carrying our full trays to our table, Gary and I were engrossed in conversation . . . when someone sideswiped Gary and his tray. Within a split second, Gary's huge, messy meal had landed all over his pants and shoes. With tremendous anger and vitriol, Gary reacted by yelling in the direction of the person who banged into him, "Are you *an idiot*?!"

When the person turned around, Gary and I painfully realized: No, she wasn't "an idiot"; she was *blind*!

Gary and I apologized profusely to that young lady. She was kind enough to forgive us and said that the collision was her fault. That day, I learned a valuable lesson about the importance of *understanding* where other relevant individuals are coming from *before* making an unthinking, destructive, emotion-filled life choice regarding them, and then acting on it.

Toxic-Energy-Charge Dissipation is a process whereby you become able—through deep self-exploration, as well as an understanding of others—to more easily diffuse and thereby diminish the power of the awesome energy charges generated from your highly toxic and deeply embedded emotions. This scenario is analogous to sprinkling rock salt on deeply frozen ice. The salt melts the ice, just as understanding, respect, compassion, forgiveness, and love can melt a deeply frozen heart, soul, and psyche. The result is that once the ice is sufficiently melted, it is far easier to chip away, break up, and remove it from your driveway or sidewalk. Similarly, with effective exploration and respectful understanding and compassion, your deeply held hurt, pain, and defenses can be melted and chipped away, so that their power and intense pull are significantly dissipated.

Throughout the rest of our discussions of *Step 4B*, there will be illustrations of how understanding, respect, empathy, compassion, forgiveness, and love are tremendously effective *Toxic-Energy-Charge Dissipaters*, as well as a great help in enabling you to break the chains of some of your most deeply embedded *Destructive, Emotion-Triggered Scripting*.

"CARLA"—A CASE OF *GENERATIONAL, DESTRUCTIVE, EMOTION-TRIGGERED SCRIPTING*

Let's go back to the case of Carla, whom I have not yet counseled. As you will remember, Carla perceived that she had been abandoned by everyone who mattered in her life. As a result, she developed some highly toxic, self-destructive behavioral scripts in order to protect her *Heart-of-Hearts* from experiencing any more feelings of abandonment, rejection, disappointment, hurt, and pain.

Should I have the opportunity to work with Carla, my goals, through the process of *Toxic-Energy-Charge Dissipation*, would be to:

1. Help her to clearly see and consciously *understand* the poisonous, *Generational, Emotion-Triggered Scripting* that has taken place and that has very possibly been genetically passed down to her, as well as how her exposure to this scripting and other unconscious subsequent influences has victimized her; and to

2. Help her break the generational-scripting chain, so that she'll no longer unconsciously react in response to her feelings and perceptions of always feeling abandoned, betrayed, and not worthy of love by in turn passing on the scripting and thereby:

   a. abandoning or betraying others;

   b. withdrawing her love and compassion from others;

   c. not permitting herself to accept the gifts of love and compassion from others, or to give them to others; and

   d. being so controlling, rigid, and protective of her heart, soul, psyche, and well-being that she doesn't dare open her *Heart-of-Hearts* to the many blessings that she does possess and can enjoy in the future.

Because Carla's poisonous feelings are so deeply entrenched in her *Heart-of-Hearts*; the energy charges from those feelings are so very potent; and her defenses are so firmly locked in place, *Regular-Strength, Toxic-Energy-Charge Dissipation* may not effectively remedy the problem. As a result, she may well need to work with a qualified individual with whom she is in simpatico. This professional can help her to understand and appreciate her history and how she is negatively scripted by it. By doing this, she can then begin to dissipate her highly toxic energy charges.

Some steps that I would take to dissipate the tremendous power of Carla's potentially destructive energy charges would be to:

1. Discuss with Carla the poisonous generational scripting that she has been subjected to and influenced by throughout her life, so that she clearly *sees* it and *understands* the deleterious effects that it has had on her and her family members;

2. Have her *understand* that this scripting consists of her perceiving and feeling that she has been or is being *abandoned*, *betrayed*, and *unloved*; and that she, in turn, has adopted the script of abandoning and betraying others and withdrawing her love from them;

3. Discuss how her very potent and deeply imbedded emotion-generated energy charges overtake, overpower, and thereby negate her ability to think, reason, and act according to her best judgment at *Crunch Time!*; instead, she unthinkingly and destructively reacts out of feelings of deep pain, hurt, rejection, unlovability, and anger when she makes many of her critical life choices;

4. Have her absorb and fully understand and appreciate that some highly toxic *Generational, Destructive, Emotion-Triggered Scripting* has left a number of her family members

angry, bitter, hateful, lonely, empty, pathetic, and CAN-CER-FILLED;

5. Have her realize that she does not want to be like those angry, bitter, CANCER-FILLED or spiritually empty, lost family members;

(I focus on the fact that many of Carla's emotionally poisoned family members let their inner anger and rage fester within them to such a degree that they became cancer victims, because I know that Carla dearly cherishes her health and physical well-being. If I could help her to clearly understand that contracting a life-threatening disease may well be the result of allowing toxic scripts to continue to poison her *Heart-of-Hearts*, hopefully the incredibly potent energy charges from Carla wanting to maintain her great health [a very pure piece of her *Gold* and a highly potent *PET*] will generate the motivation and power for her to break free from the chain of her destructive scripting.)[12]

6. Help Carla to recognize that her forbears were also poisonously scripted and victimized, and therefore, they were not aware or in control of their behavior; they, too, needed and/ or still need *understanding* and *compassion*;

7. Enable Carla to realize and embrace that she so very much needs to *forgive* her forbears and current family members, for they know not what they have done or are doing, respectively, just as she knew not what she was doing. (Hopefully,

---

12 This is analogous to my dad telling my mom that she was "mean" when she made him wait for her for over two hours outside a restaurant before their theatre date. For my mom, being called "mean" struck her so deeply—because it implied that she was acting like her "mean" mother, whom she loathed—that it broke up my mom's destructive-scripting blockage. She was then able to see, think, and act clearly . . . and no longer be late or be perceived as "mean."

she, too, will be forgiven by those whom she has negatively scripted and hurt deeply!);

8. Have her understand that by putting a definitive end to this self-sabotaging scripting, she can grow to become someone who can love and be compassionate, and also develop into someone who feels that she is truly worthy of receiving love and compassion; I would also focus on Carla's being able to truly and fully love and be loved, because buried under all of the festering feelings of anger, hurt, rejection, and unlovability is someone who desperately craves love and wants to give love in return (Carla's purest and most potent *Gold*);

9. Have Carla understand, absorb, and be thoroughly energized by the fact that notwithstanding all of the pain, hurt, rejection, and heartache that she has endured, she absolutely has THE POWER—literally the requisite high-voltage energy charges—to put a real end to her destructive scripting and its devastating effects. One way to most effectively drive this point home is to suggest that she emulate the highly constructive actions of her "Aunt Zelda," whom she loves and looks up to as a mother figure. Zelda was subject to the same poisonous generational scripting as was Charisse, Zelda's sister and Carla's mother. However, because Zelda, at a very early age, was able to effectively evaluate and understand how very destructive and self-sabotaging acting out her mother's destructive scripting would be, she made a well considered, resolute choice *not* to follow the same poisonous paths as did her mother. Through seeking and securing effective therapy, over time, Zelda built and nurtured a warm and loving family around her—a family that Carla has said she wishes that she had, both growing up and with Ryan, her former husband; (Additional Carla *Gold*!);

10. Explain to Carla and have her absorb and appreciate that she is blessed to be a beautiful, fit, very smart, multi-talented woman who can have a great life ahead of her—in fact, the love-filled life that she craves—if she follows *The 7 Steps of Emotion Mastery*; and

11. Explain to Carla that if she opens her *Heart-of-Hearts* and her perspective on things, her children will want nothing more than to love her and be there with and for her. (Her purest *Gold* and strongest *PET*.) And if she grows and evolves into an open, loving, forgiving, compassionate, giving, appreciative person—which she absolutely CAN accomplish—she will be much more ready to have a loving, healthy relationship with the right man, and that man will be much more likely to gravitate toward and grow to love her in return, and this time, *stay with* (and not *abandon*) her. (More Carla *Gold*!)

As we have discussed, once the dissipation of her toxic energy charges has been accomplished, the chances are far greater that Carla's *Frisuals* will overpower and negate the potentially poisonous energy charges that trigger her toxic scripts. This would allow Carla to much more easily break free of the *Destructive, Emotion-Generated Scripting* that has poisoned her *Heart-of-Hearts*, her most important relationships, and her life. The key here is for Carla to secure the help of someone qualified to help her see, understand, and appreciate how her destructive, generational scripting is sabotaging her.

Your *Take-Aways:*

1. With knowledge, understanding, and appreciation of your own background, as well as that of relevant family members, you can begin to dissipate the extremely potent energy charges that flood you at *Crunch Time!*.

2. If you can clearly see and truly appreciate how your *Destructive, Emotion-Triggered Scripting* has negatively affected your life, as well as the lives of others you care about, you have taken a big step toward breaking free from the scripts that sabotage you.

"CASSIE"—*GENERATIONAL, DESTRUCTIVE, EMOTION-TRIGGERED SCRIPTING*, CONTINUED

I was recently introduced to Cassie, whose *Generational, Destructive, Emotion-Triggered Scripting* is somewhat similar to that of Carla's, which we just discussed. However, the highly self-destructive acts engaged in by Cassie are in many ways far more serious. Here is Cassie's profoundly painful family background:

Cassie lives in an East Coast city. She is a seventeen-year-old girl with three older brothers. One of these brothers, "Sam," is substantially older than Cassie and is her best friend. He is the only long-term, loving, nurturing, care-giving figure in her life, and for all intents and purposes, he raised her. Sam is very happily married to a wonderfully warm and giving woman, "Kerri." Cassie has a grandmother, "Lucy," who literally abandoned her daughter "Maria" (Cassie's mother), when Maria was six months old. Sam says that a relative told him that Lucy may well have suffered from some form of chemical imbalance. Throughout Maria's childhood, Maria received no love or nurturing from either her mother or the people with whom she lived.

When Maria was eighteen years old, she married "William." She openly admits that the only reason she married him was to escape from her horrible life in a foster home. During the ensuing five years after her marriage, Maria gave birth to four children, with Cassie being the youngest.

According to Sam, Maria has always been "ice-cold" and cruel to Cassie. In fact, Sam doesn't recall their mother *ever* holding, hugging, or kissing Cassie. To this day, whenever someone tries to hug Cassie, her body instantly becomes rigid, and she shakes. Sam says that from the moment Cassie was born, she was psychologically, emotionally, and physically abandoned by her mother. What makes matters worse is that Sam and his two brothers somehow managed to receive "a bit of nurturing and support" from Maria. Sam believes that this preferential treatment is a reflection of the fact that in Maria's culture, boys are put on pedestals. Cassie sadly puts it this way: "The boys are treated like princes; and I'm treated like Cinderella!"

During further discussions with Sam, I learned that in certain situations, Maria can trigger blinding, rage-filled reactions from Cassie. Literally! Apparently, Cassie's anger runs so deep and is so ugly that at times, she can't see straight and loses all ability to act rationally. It also triggers highly self-destructive actions. In one instance, after Maria evoked a rage-filled response from the fifteen-year-old Cassie, Cassie immediately got herself pregnant with a child she conceived with her physically and emotionally abusive boyfriend. Some time after that, as a reaction to Maria's cold and totally uncaring behavior, Cassie attempted suicide. But immediately after taking enough sleeping pills "to kill a horse," she called Sam, who rushed her to the hospital.

Recently, when Maria acted in a manner that showed absolutely no regard for Cassie's feelings or for her well-being, Cassie flew into a rage, lashing out at everyone around her—including Sam. Soon thereafter, Cassie went into a department store and was caught attempting to steal clothing. When Maria was asked to go down to the police station to clear her daughter so that charges wouldn't be filed against Cassie, Maria allegedly refused, supposedly answering, "Let them lock her up! I'm not going to help her!" It was Sam who had to rush down to the station, smooth things over with the store owner, and rescue Cassie.

From all of this, it is clear that:

1. Cassie has been abandoned in almost every meaningful way by her mother. As a result, deep feelings of hurt, hopelessness, unlovability, rejection, and betrayal are deeply embedded in her *Heart-of-Hearts*. When these feelings are ignited, powerful feelings of anger and rage are triggered; this results in Cassie repeatedly acting out the scripts of self-sabotage, lashing out at others, and being devastatingly self-destructive;

2. By getting pregnant, by attempting to commit suicide, and by getting caught stealing jewelry, Cassie is obviously crying out for her mother to act in a loving, caring, concerned manner toward her—which Maria *never* does! As a result, Cassie's intense feelings of rejection, which are triggered by her repeated disappointments, in turn lead to more and deeper feelings of hopelessness, unlovability, and rock-bottom, low self-esteem; and

3. Cassie's situation needs remedying as soon as possible before she engages in her next rage-driven, self-destructive action, the damage from which could be irreparable or even fatal.

It was immediately after Cassie committed the attempted robbery that Sam asked for my advice. Upon receiving all of this information, my first thought was that Cassie needed to see both a good neurologist and a psychiatrist in order to learn whether some form of chemical disorder was exacerbating her reactions. Sam said that he would make these appointments right away. In the meantime, he asked me to see what I could do to help his sister. Unquestionably, my initial work with Cassie—should we collaborate—would involve major *Toxic-Energy-Charge Dissipation*, as she has some very deep-seated and potentially poisonous feelings embedded in her *Heart-of-Hearts* that have been generating extremely powerful energy charges. These charges would need some immediate, substantial dissipation.

During some initial talks, Cassie recounted her background to me at first in a very protective way, and later, in a more open, emotional manner. The relevant events she shared closely mirrored those given to me by Sam. My first goal would be to have Cassie truly understand *why* her mother acts the way she does, and that her mother's behavior has nothing to do with Cassie; but rather that it is all about Maria's love-less upbringing. Through acquiring consciousness, understanding, and appreciation of the horrific childhood her mother has been through, hopefully Cassie would develop compassion for her mother, initially on an intellectual level. And in time, as soon as she is able and psychologically and emotionally ready, she can then absorb and embrace these concepts on an emotional level. As this is accomplished, assuming there is no chemically caused impediment, Cassie's heretofore extremely potent, poisonous energy charges can begin to dissipate. For our purposes in studying the process of *Toxic-Energy-Charge Dissipation*, I will outline four means of energy-charge dissipation for Cassie:

1. Cassie needs to clearly see and appreciate intellectually, and then emotionally, that her mother was abandoned at six months old and never received any love, care, attention, or nurturing...ever! Due to this devastating experience, her mother is incapable of loving others; and it is in no way a

reflection of Cassie's lovability, likeability, gifts, abilities, or potential. Nor is this horrible reality any of Cassie's fault or doing. It is clear that much or all of this damage was wrought years ago, when her mother was physically, psychologically, and emotionally abandoned as a child. Therefore, it is absolutely necessary for Cassie to *understand* Maria's loveless and uncaring behavior in light of Maria's truly heartbreaking, rage-filled childhood.

Hopefully, by gaining this key understanding, Cassie can grow to have *compassion* for her mother and *forgive* her, despite the fact that her mother, at this point, is still incapable of truly loving or giving to Cassie. One major byproduct of Cassie developing understanding, compassion, and forgiveness is that some substantial energy-charge dissipation will take place;

2. It is essential (1) for Cassie to no longer engage in self-destructive acts in an effort to secure a positive, loving reaction from her mother; and (2) for Cassie to stop suffering heart-, soul-, and psyche-destroying disappointments in connection with her mother. In order to do this, Cassie must understand, as well as intellectually and emotionally accept, that trying to elicit the love that she seeks from her mother is as likely as Cassie drawing blood from a stone. It's not going to happen! Furthermore, Cassie will always be profoundly disappointed if she has any expectations of eliciting her mother's love.

Obviously, this is an extremely painful realization for Cassie to intellectually and emotionally absorb and accept; but when she does, she hopefully will no longer put herself in harm's way in an effort to secure the near impossible: her mother's unconditional love.

Once again, this process is designed to dissipate Cassie's extremely potent, poisonous, emotion-generated energy charges so that she can truly begin to master *The 7 Steps of Emotion Mastery*;

3. I will meet with Cassie's mother to learn whether any counseling of Maria can dissipate the deeply embedded feelings of hurt, pain, rejection, and unlovability that are in Maria's *Heart-of-Hearts*. If some dissipation can indeed be accomplished, maybe Maria, in time, can gradually grow to be a (somewhat) loving, caring, and nurturing mother to Cassie. Any payoff here will certainly be worth the effort!

   Additionally, when Cassie is psychologically and emotionally ready, with sincere *compassion* and her own long-stifled love, she could start to show her mother what love is by giving love, warmth, and caring to her love-starved mother. By effectively doing this, the ice in both of their mutually love-starved hearts could start to melt away, which would begin to reverse the chain of their poisonous, generational scripting; and

4. I will make sure that Sam and Kerri will "be there" as much as possible for Cassie during this difficult and all-important time, as they are the only loving constants in Cassie's life. Additionally, if Cassie has any other loving and supportive relatives or friends, they should also be asked to be there for and with Cassie. The aim here is to begin to instill warm feelings of love, caring, treasuring, lovability, worthiness, and high self-esteem in place of the many poison-evoking emotions that are lodged in Cassie's *Heart-of-Hearts*. All of this can help to dissipate the highly potent, poisonous energy charges that have triggered Cassie's self-destructive behavior.

Your *Take-Away:*

By *understanding* and feeling *compassion* for, as well as *forgiving*, poisonously scripted individuals who have hurt you, you can dissipate the poisonous high-voltage energy charges that are triggered within your *Heart-of-Hearts* at *Crunch Time!*. When this has been accomplished, you are far more likely to make *Golden* and *Truthful* life choices in lieu of ones that are self-sabotaging.

"PHILIP"—UTILIZING YOUR EMOTIONAL TRIGGERS TO BREAK THE CHAIN OF YOUR *GENERATIONAL, DESTRUCTIVE, EMOTION-TRIGGERED SCRIPTING*

Philip sought my help because he was unable to control his flash temper. Among Philip's various anger-related challenges was his egregious road-rage. In one instance, Philip became so incensed when a driver cut him off that he purposely and menacingly tailgated the perpetrator for over twenty minutes. According to Philip, he wound up going about five miles out of his way to "really scare the guy."

In another instance, Philip was shopping for Christmas gifts with his wife, "Jan." In the underground mall parking lot, there were far more drivers looking for spaces than there were spaces available. Thankfully, after about a half hour of Philip and Jan driving around "like rats caught in a maze"—and with Philip's patience growing thinner by the second—they saw someone walk up and open the trunk of the car right in front of them. Eureka! The Promised Land was before them! As Philip and Jan painstakingly waited for the driver to unload her wagon full of purchases into the trunk and then strap her child into her car seat, Philip once again grew impatient. Then, finally, the woman got into her car, turned on the ignition, and began to pull out of her spot. But, just as Philip stepped on the gas, "some woman" who was driving by saw the space and in one lightning-quick move, swooped in and took Philip and Jan's spot. Within an instant, enraged beyond reason, Philip jumped out of the car and began yelling every unrepeatable obscenity imaginable. The woman, fearing for her life, stayed in her locked car as Philip violently rapped on her car door, threatening to beat the "bleep" out of her!

With mall security and Jan trying to do all they could to calm Philip down, he suddenly felt a heavy chest pain. The attack brought him to his knees. Jan, fearing that Philip was having a heart attack, almost had one herself. Soon thereafter, Philip was taken to the local hospital, where he was fortunately diagnosed with a less serious angina attack. It was after this incident that Philip and Jan asked for my help.

Upon meeting Philip, I could see that for the most part, he had a really warm, outgoing personality. From what I gleaned and learned from others, he was a loving father and an attentive husband. The issue appeared to be that whenever he felt that he was wronged or disrespected, he would uncontrollably explode (much like Leslie, whom we discussed earlier). Jan confided to me that it was as if Philip anticipated being, or expected to be, disrespected, and when he actually got what he sought or expected, "Something would go off in him. You could see it in his eyes. All of a sudden, he'd be consumed with a burning, seething anger." As a result, Jan's (and Philip's) big fear was that one day, Philip would get "tweaked" and in an unthinking, emotionally charged response, do something terrible to himself or to the person who wronged him.

Prior to beginning our discussions, I explained to Philip and Jan that along with my counseling, Philip should see a qualified neurologist to learn if his mood swings were caused by a chemical imbalance or other chemical abnormality.

We began by my asking Philip to carefully think about *why* he became so enraged when he was wronged or dissed, and *why* he felt compelled to exact retribution against the offender. After he shared his initial thoughts, I asked him to take as much time as was necessary over the next few days or weeks in order for him to figure out where all of his anger comes from.

About two-and-a-half weeks later, Philip responded that he felt that when people disrespected him—which angered him "to no end"—they needed to pay for it. Essentially, since they inflicted some form of psychological, emotional, or physical pain on him, he should retaliate in kind.

I then asked him to carefully focus on the reasons *why* he felt that he needed to respond so violently when he felt disrespected. Philip answered that he had talked at length with Jan about this, and "all" he could come up with was that his father always hit him with both his hand and his belt buckle, and that his father never listened to him or respected what he had to say or who he was. He despised his father for this.

"O.K.!," I thought. "It doesn't take the likes of Freud, Erikson, or Jung to figure out where at least some of Philip's rage stems from. The challenge here is that the energy charges generated from Philip's seething anger/rage were tremendously strong and when triggered, almost always disabled his ability to think and reason clearly. Therefore, in order to significantly weaken those mega-potent, potentially toxic energy charges and then overpower them, we first needed to dissipate the energy charges from his toxic, generational scripting."

With this *Step* in mind, Philip's next homework assignment was to take as much time as necessary to compile his *Gold/Truth List*.

He took almost three weeks to make his *List*:

1. to be a person of God and to do His work;

2. to be a good, loving father and husband;

3. to make life choices anger/rage-free so that they reflect what he truly wants to accomplish;

4. to have a warm, loving family and home environment;

5. to treat his children the absolute opposite way that he was treated as a child; that is, to treat them with love and respect, and not with disrespect, violence, or intimidation;

6. to be rid of the burning anger/hatred within him, and to live a life of peace; and

7. to continue to grow at his firm, so that he can provide the financial stability that his father never gave him or his siblings.

Before discussing Philip's *Gold/Truth* with him, I needed to diffuse a good deal of the potency of his potentially sabotaging energy charges. (Some focused *Toxic-Energy-Charge Dissipation*.) So we discussed, at great length, the following:

1. We will assume for the sake of our explorations that the individuals who were the target of Philip's anger were in fact rude and/or disrespectful to him; and

2. It would be a tragedy if Philip allowed these offenders' bad behavior to trigger behavior from Philip that would be devastatingly damaging to him (such as getting a heart attack or worse as a result of his anger/rage) and/or to the individuals—his wife and children—whom he dearly loves (such as losing Philip because of a fatal heart attack or his going to jail for physically assaulting someone).

During our talks, I made sure that Philip absorbed and appreciated the possibly devastating consequences of his potential, destructive actions. (He became *Consequence Cognizant*.) In time, Philip wholeheartedly agreed that in the big picture, seeking retribution against a rude or disrespectful individual wasn't at all worth the horrific risk of losing his health, life, freedom, self-respect, family, and job! (His *PETS*.) Additionally, he concurred that his purest *Gold* of "being a person of God" meant walking away from the perpetrators—not seeking to harm them.

I then explained to Philip that he indeed had the power to mold his behavior in a manner that is consistent with what he truly wants (his *Gold*) and who he aspires to be (his *Truth*). A clear and shining example of this was how he *consciously chose* to break the chain of the *Generational, Destructive, Emotion-Triggered Scripting* that he was subjected to, in that both his grandfather and father were physically, mentally, and emotionally abusive to their children. Philip had been able to effectively break the chain of that emotionally charged, horrible behavior by *consciously choosing* to be a warm, loving, respectful parent—who is never violent with his children.

So, if Philip could consciously choose and successfully implement this positive parental behavioral strategy and thereby nullify his poisonous generational scripting once, he could most certainly do the same in response to individuals who he perceives disrespect him. Essentially, this is simply another chain of *Generational, Destructive, Emotion-Triggered Scripting* for him to break.

After Philip fully acknowledged, appreciated, and felt his power to be a chain breaker, we once again went over—and this time, Philip much more fully bought into—the following three energy-charge-dissipating concepts, which prominently incorporated his *PETS* and abilities:

1. It is in NO WAY WORTH RISKING his FREEDOM, FAMILY, PHYSICAL WELL-BEING, and HEALTH by expressing his anger when someone knowingly or unknowingly is disrespectful to him or pushes his emotional buttons;

2. As a "PERSON OF GOD" who wants "to do His work," he must walk away from a potentially destructive or

self-sabotaging situation instead of being emotionally pulled into it; and

3. He has the POWER, which he has successfully tapped into and used before, to break a sabotaging chain of generational, destructive scripting. Therefore, he must once again draw upon that power in order to BREAK ANOTHER potentially LIFE-THREATENING, CAREER-ENDING, FAMILY-DAMAGING CHAIN.

During our next meeting, I asked Philip if he agreed that the anger and vitriol that his grandfather unleashed on his father—and that his father, in turn, subjected him to—was a reflection of the festering, profound pain, suffering, and rage that they felt within. Philip thought about this and agreed that "it *definitely* was!"

I then said, "If you truly feel as if you need to see the offenders 'pay' for their bad acts, always be aware that their bad acts are a reflection of how badly they feel about themselves. And rest assured, these individuals feel horribly. So Philip, don't worry! They're stewing in their own ugly, vitriolic, painful, loathsome juices."

Knowing that deep down, Philip is a compassionate person and truly wants to take the God-like path, I waited a moment and then suggested the following idea: "Philip, I have a far better and more evolved solution. Instead of being angry with those who wrong you and seeking any karmic or other form of retribution, you might want to understand them; feel compassion for them; and empathize with them, as their bad behavior reflects the extreme hurt, pain, and anger lodged in their souls."

As time went on and Philip thought more and more about this concept, I could sense Philip's heart opening as he began to feel *compassion*—a beautiful feeling . . . and a very effective *Toxic-Energy-Charge Dissipater*.

My goal during our talks was for Philip to not only no longer feel the need to *express* his anger/rage, but, even more importantly, to no longer *feel* anger in these situations, as "grudges ultimately hurt the ones who hold them."[E] In order to accomplish this, my goal was to have Philip grow to be *understanding, compassionate,* and *sympathetic/empathetic,* as these feelings and gifts can melt and eventually warm even the coldest heart. Fortunately, this eventually happened with Philip.

I further explained to Philip that even the mere feeling of anger can cause severe, and in some cases irreparable, internal damage, and that he was very lucky to have gotten away with just an angina attack in the parking lot, as opposed to a heart attack. So allowing these individuals and their bad acts to trigger any degree of anger within him isn't healthy for *him*! What *is* healthy is to view these irksome acts and their perpetrators with *understanding* and *compassion* . . . and to let them go!

We concluded our initial set of conversations, with my using Philip's purest *Gold* and strongest *PETS* to help compel him to let another person's inappropriate or rude behavior roll right off him. I continued by doing my best to drive home this thought: "Philip, always remember: If you want to be a person of God, isn't being understanding, compassionate, and sympathetic/empathetic the God-like thing to do in these circumstances?"

"Yes! It absolutely is!" Philip openheartedly agreed.

Over time, I saw a significant change in Philip's perspective on things. He truly wanted to once again break his generational, destructive, emotional-scripting chain and to be "a person of God," as well as the loving husband and father that he envisioned in his *Gold* and *Truth Lists.* Our talks effectively dissipated a very significant amount of the power generated from Philip's emotional scripting. As a result, he and I were then able to construct his *Prevent Offense* and his *Frisuals*, with the excellent outcome being that at *Crunch Time!*, Philip's highly potent energy charges blew away his now materially dissipated energy charges from his once potentially self-destructive emotions.

Let's review how Philip's *Toxic-Energy-Charge Dissipation* worked:

From Philip's *Gold List*, I learned that one of Philip's very strongest *PETS* was his fervent desire to be as "God-like" as possible. This implied that *compassion* for and *understanding* of others would be attractive and essential qualities for Philip to adopt as staples. He also wanted to have a loving, warm, respectful relationship with his children and be a good and healthy role model for them. This indicated that he wanted to break all of the chains of his generational scripting that produced anger, rage, vitriol, and self-destructive behavior. In fact, Philip's self-image was heavily based on his being the polar opposite of his father and grandfather, who both regularly reacted in anger and rage.

Additionally, Philip took his responsibility to be a stable parental and family force and a provider very earnestly. Therefore, it was crystal-clear to him that being put in jail, suffering a debilitating heart attack, being a poor role model for his children, and/or losing his job by expressing his rage/anger/vitriol would seriously jeopardize those things he so dearly valued.

Finally, in his *Gold List*, Philip said that he fervently wanted to eliminate the strong feelings of anger, rage, and hurt lodged in his *Heart-of-Hearts*. One effective way to do this is to push out all of the feelings of hurt, pain, rejection, hopelessness, and disrespect suffered at the hands of his father and grandfather and substitute, in their place, love, kindness, caring, understanding, empathy, sympathy, and the exceedingly positive, self-esteem-building feelings of being a person who consistently feels and expresses—all God-like qualities.

By knowing Philip's highly-prized *Gold* and his most compelling *PETS*, I was able to get through to Philip by using values and concepts to which Philip could personally relate and by which he would be intellectually, psychologically, and emotionally moved and motivated. My *Gold*-filled ideas (which were his strongest *PETS*) so emotionally touched him and generated such potent energy charges within him that he was able to dissipate the once very powerful emotion-generated energy charges emanating from his destructive scripting. As a result, after doing his *Frisuals*, with his vision and best judgment crystal-clear, and his *Heart-of-Hearts* much fuller with the God-like qualities of understanding, compassion, and love, many of Philip's anger-related problems were behind him.

Your *Take-Aways:*

1. By understanding your background and appreciating how your *Generational, Destructive, Emotion-Triggered Scripting* has negatively affected your choices and behaviors, you can dissipate the high-voltage, poisonous energy charges that flood you and lead you to make self-sabotaging choices.

2. By knowing your most potent *Gold* and *Truth*, which are your *PETS*, and effectively utilizing them, you can dissipate poisonous energy charges and be an effective generational, destructive-script chain breaker!

Your 2 *Crunch Time!* Steps

STEP 5

When Possible,
Review Your *Crunch Time! Reminder List*

Step 5

This *Step* is optional, depending upon the amount of time that you have between when you recognize that you are faced with making a life choice and when you must make it.

Ideally, you will have enough time to go over your *Reminder List* and thereby significantly increase the likelihood that you will make a *Golden/Truthful* life choice. If the end result of your choice is profound or life-changing—and you want to *Come Up BIG!*—then it behooves you to take the time to carefully go over your *Reminder List* before making your choice.

Here's your *Crunch Time! Reminder List* in skeletal form:

Reminder #1: You want complete *intellectual clarity* and *precision* when you make your life choice(s).

Reminder #2: Remember and vividly visualize when you made self-diminishing, destructive, and self-sabotaging life choices in the past, and how very dissatisfying/horrible these choices turned out.

Reminder #3: Identify your most potent *PETS*.

Reminder #4: Amp up your *PETS* by bundling them.

Reminder #5: Dissipate your potentially toxic energy charges.

Reminder #6: Be *Consequence Cognizant*!

Reminder #7: Ask yourself: "What do I *truly* want to accomplish with this life choice?"; and "What kind of a person do I *truly* want to be?"

Reminder #8: Make a *Blessing List*.

Reminder #9: Go over what you have prepared yourself to do at *Crunch Time!* during your *Prevent Offense*. Cognitively click into:

> a. the *specific* or *general* life choice(s) that you've prepared yourself to make at *Crunch Time!*; and
>
> b. the *Frame(s)* and *visual(s)* that you've prepared, so that you can now make a *Truthful* and *Golden* life choice.

Additionally, make sure that before you make your life choice, your *Gold* and *Truth* haven't changed since you last prepared or reviewed your *Prevent Offense*, and that no new data, which need to be considered, have entered into the *Crunch Time!* picture.

Now, let's discuss the *Crunch Time! Reminder Checklist* so that the *Reminders* are more memorable.

Reminder #1: First and foremost, make sure that you DO NOT make an important life choice when you are angry, enraged, fearful, hurt, or needy; or when you feel rejected, hopeless, betrayed, or emotionally "off," until you can calm down, relax, and can think and reason clearly as you go through your *Crunch Time! Reminder Checklist.*

Always remember that there is tremendous potential that if you unthinkingly react by making an important life choice when you are angry, enraged, fearful, hurt, or needy; or when you feel rejected, hopeless, or emotionally "off-balance," that choice will result in your taking a self-destructive or self-sabotaging action. Prime examples of this unfortunate result can be seen in the case of both Leslie and Beth, whom we discussed earlier. In Leslie's case, she was so *enraged* by how she felt about her management "shafting" her that she lashed out and lost her wonderful job, and in doing so, she embroiled herself in a long-term contract with an ineffective talent representative whom she would later describe as "despicable."

These horrible things happened because at *Crunch Time!*, Leslie made two life choices and acted upon them when she and her intellect were flooded with high-voltage energy charges generated by poisonous emotions. Knowing Leslie as I now do, had she been exposed to *The 7 Steps of Emotion Mastery*, I am sure that she would still have her job today.

In Beth's case, you will recall that despite her clearly knowing that her love interest, Kent, needed "air" and "space" until he was ready to be in a serious romantic relationship, she kept pressing for more attention and commitment and thereby smothered him into retreat.

In hindsight, when Beth could see things in a calmer, clearer manner, she realized and acknowledged that she did the *one* thing that she *knowingly* would never mean to do: push away and alienate someone with whom she very much wanted to have a long-term relationship. Because Beth was overcome with energy charges generated by her feelings of love, hurt, insecurity, hopelessness, unlovability, and rejection, her best judgment and sound reasoning processes were dismantled at *Crunch Time!;* as a direct result, she chose to act in a totally self-sabotaging manner.

Reminder #1:

DO NOT make a life choice when you are flooded with poisonous-emotion-generated energy charges, or when you feel emotionally "off-balance."

Reminder #2: Vividly recall and objectively review the self-defeating and self-sabotaging choices that you made the last time or the previous times you felt as you do now (angry, enraged, disrespected, fearful, hurt, betrayed, needy, rejected, and/or hopeless) and what you did when you were faced with the same or a similar situation. ("I reacted out of anger, rage, hurt, need, rejection, and/or fear.") Then choose a more positive, self-enhancing course of action.

Let's go back to the situations of Leslie, Bill, Brandon, and Beth. One thing these individuals have in common is a *recurring pattern* of making a life choice and thereafter acting the same exact way (their script) when faced with the same or a similar situation.

1. In Leslie's case, whenever she felt disrespected by her management, she would immediately lash out and take a retaliatory action directed at them;

2. In Bill's case, whenever someone at work would push his emotional buttons, it would trigger one of his vicious, vitriolic verbal attacks;

3. In Brandon's case, every time a woman would become comfortable enough to begin a sexual relationship with him, his urge or compulsion to have sex to pornography flooded

his psyche. As a result, he couldn't have or enjoy having sex without it;

4. In Beth's case, her uncontrollable poisonous energy charges caused her to repeatedly come on way too strong with her love interests at inappropriate times.

As we now know, the extremely negative outcomes of the above individuals' emotionally triggered, self-sabotaging behavioral patterns were as follows:

1. Leslie continued to poison her relationship with her management until she finally lost her highly coveted, lucrative job as a star of a daytime soap opera;

2. Bill lost jobs, including the position he loved at a highly prestigious firm;

3. Brandon alienated and lost all of the women whom he was interested in, including Kelly, who he believed was the "absolute love of his life"; and

4. Beth drove away all of her love interests, including Kent, with whom she felt a "true connection."

In all of these cases, there is bad news and good. The bad news: These destructive behavioral patterns repeatedly resulted in these individuals being flooded with highly potent energy charges, which dismantled their best judgment and reasoning processes at *Crunch Time!*. As a result, Leslie, Bill, Brandon, and Beth suffered heartbreaking/demoralizing setbacks. The good news: Because there is a *clear* pattern of repeated (self-destructive) behavior, through honest, objective self-exploration, these individuals can identify the sabotaging pattern of behavior and take the appropriate *7 Steps* in order to put an end to it. Additionally, for the most part, people tend to *repeat* self-destructive behavior, as potentially poisonous emotions embedded in their *Heart-of-Hearts* are just that—embedded. As a result, they stay there unless and until you take steps to remedy the situation. Therefore, in all likelihood, you will often have the *gift* of previous instances of destructive behavior to use in openly and honestly recalling, reviewing, and constructively changing.

So, let's complete this *Reminder* using Leslie, Bill, and Beth to illustrate how to make the most of the processes of "Recall," "Review," and "Constructive Change."

If there is a "next time," and Leslie receives a (new) contract offer; and her feelings of hurt, disrespect, and anger are triggered, she would immediately:

1. *Recall*: Remember that there were a number of instances when her former management did things that made her feel angry, sad, hurt, disrespected, and/or "shafted."

2. *Review*: Acknowledge, understand, and appreciate that in the past, she acted out of blinding emotion, to her detriment. In hindsight, when she was poisonous-emotion-free, she would realize that she could have thought and reasoned things out far more clearly and could have made more constructive choices.

3. *Constructive Change*: As a result, starting with *next Crunch Time!* and moving forward, she will *choose* not to react out of emotion, but instead will make well thought-out choices that are consistent with her *Gold* and *Truth*. In this case, Leslie will make sure that she doesn't do anything to risk losing a new job or (irreparably) alienating her new management.

When Bill's emotional buttons are pushed by someone in the workplace, he would immediately:

1. *Recall*: Remember that there have been a number of instances at work when he has lost control of his temper, which resulted in his best judgment being disabled.

2. *Review*: Acknowledge, understand, and appreciate that in the past, every time that he became emotionally flooded with high-voltage, anger-generated energy charges, he put his job and livelihood in jeopardy; and that ultimately, his anger-filled outbursts cost him his job. Twice! In poison-ous-emotion-free hindsight, he would realize that he could have handled things far differently and much more con-structively.

3. *Constructive Change*: As a result, starting with *next Crunch Time!* and moving forward, Bill will *choose* not to react out of emotion, but instead will make a well thought-out choice that is consistent with his *Gold* and *Truth*. He will opt to never express his anger in the workplace or mistreat staff members, and thereby risk losing his job.

When Beth is beginning to date someone, and her feelings of love, insecurity, neediness, and/or hopelessness surface, she would imme-diately:

1. *Recall*: Remember that there has been a pattern of her intensely liking someone whom she begins to date, which triggers certain emotion-generated energy charges that cause her to unthinkingly smother and/or try to control her love-interest and their relationship status.

2. *Review*: Acknowledge, understand, and appreciate that in the past, the energy charges from her poisonous emotions flooded and dismantled her best judgment and reasoning

processes. As a result, she repeatedly pushed men away in whom she was interested. The results of this self-sabotaging behavior caused her tremendous feelings of pain, hurt, sadness, inadequacy, and hopelessness; which, in turn, made her poisonous energy charges *that much stronger* the next time she'd meet a man in whom she was interested. In hindsight, when she was free and clear of her poisonous emotion-generated energy charges, she would realize that she should have kept her emotions in check, giving her love-interests the space and time that they needed.

3. *Constructive Change*: As a result, starting with *next Crunch Time!* and moving forward, she will *choose* to act in a manner that will reflect her *Gold* by holding her feelings in check and letting her love-interests breathe. This way, she will give a highly valued new relationship its best shot to grow organically.

Reminder #2:

Before making a life choice, objectively review your relevant, past self-sabotaging choices when you felt as you do now (angry, hurt, sad, insecure, hopeless, rejected, and/or "off-balance"). The key for you is to make sure that you clearly see how, in the past, you have made a self-destructive choice when you and your intellect were flooded with poisonous energy charges. Your goal here is to break away from the patterns or missteps of the past, choose a more constructive course of action, and *this time*—and in the future—make a *Golden/Truthful* life choice.

Reminder #3: Identify your *PETS*. This *Reminder* asks you to identify your *most* potent *Gold* and *Truth*, which comprise *Your PETS*. For example, let's review Danielle's *Prevent-Offense Gold* and *Truth List*:

1. to provide a reliable, consistent means of support for her son, Patrick and for herself;

2. to remain in her real-estate business; and

3. to not be forced to settle for taking a boring corporate office job, which she has no interest in and doesn't find stimulating in the least.

Replay in your mind the *Gold* and *Truth* that you deemed most potent when you prepared your *Prevent Offense*.

Reminder #3:

Identify your most potent *PETS*.

Reminder #4: Amp up your *Frame(s)*™ and *visual(s)* with the supremely high-voltage energy charges of your *PETS*, so that when you *Frisual*, you put yourself in the very best position possible to overpower and thereby nullify your potentially toxic energy charges. As we've discussed, the means by which you do this is to pile on or bundle as many of your most potent *PETS* into your *Frames* and *visuals* as possible.

An excellent illustration of someone bundling her most potent *Gold* and *Truth* so as to make her *Frame* and *visual* as powerful and effective as possible is Rebeccah (please see pages 120–124). Here's another example of this process:

"Ray" suffers from acid reflux; and no matter what remedies Ray's doctors prescribed, they couldn't prevent the corrosive acid in Ray's stomach and throat from returning on a daily basis.

After battling with acid reflux for a number of years, and with Ray's throat and esophagus constantly irritated, his doctors became increasingly concerned about his contracting throat or esophageal cancer, as it ran in his family. One very big problem for Ray was that his doctors repeatedly told him that he *must* stop drinking alcohol, a warning that he couldn't get himself to heed.

Upon seeking my help, here is the super-potent bundle of *Gold* and *Truth* nuggets that we were able to compile and channel into Ray's *Frames*:

1. "BEING ALIVE AND WELL FOR MY ELEVEN-YEAR-OLD AUTISTIC CHILD, 'LUANNE,' who DESPERATELY NEEDS ME and whom I deeply love;

2. BEING ALIVE AND WELL FOR MY OTHER, OLDER CHILDREN, whom I deeply love;

3. BEING ALIVE AND WELL FOR MY MOTHER, whom I take care of and deeply love;

4. Not putting my MOTHER through the DEVASTATING PAIN OF BURYING HER ONLY CHILD;

5. Not going through the HORRIBLE, PAINFUL DISINTEGRATION that my father, uncle, and grandfather went through when they all DIED OF THROAT CANCER; and

6. Not succumbing to MY WEAKNESS/ADDICTION."

As we will discuss in *Step 6*, it was through Ray's artful bundling of his *Gold* and *Truth* that he was very soon thereafter able to begin to make positive life choices when it came to his drinking.

Reminder #4:

Amp up your *Frames* and *visuals*.

Reminder #5: Dissipate your toxic energy charges.

As you will recall, you accomplish this by using your *Toxic-Energy-Charge Dissipaters*. This means that before you make a life choice:

1. find *love* in your *Heart-of-Hearts*, and express that love in your life choice;

2. be *understanding* of yourself and of others, so that you can understand where you and others are coming from and incorporate this knowledge into your choice-making process;

3. *forgive* yourself and others in your *Heart-of-Hearts*, and manifest forgiveness when you make your life choice; and;

4. find *compassion* in your *Heart-of-Hearts*, and express your compassion.

As we found during our earlier discussion of *Toxic-Energy-Charge Dissipation*, one of the primary means of dissipating potent, negative energy charges is to *understand* and *appreciate* where *others* are coming from, so that you are truly able to *forgive* and have *compassion* for them. Here is an illustration of how *knowledge* and *understanding* of others can help to dissipate the strength and intensity of your potent negative energy charge(s):

I was deeply angry with my dad during the first few years of my life because I felt that he didn't love me. Apparently, I was so enraged when I was four years old that I threw a brick at him. Thankfully, my aim was as bad as my judgment. My deep-seated feelings of rejection, frustration, hurt, pain, and anger came from the fact that my mom was always there for me growing up. And my dad wasn't. My mom knew how to talk and relate to me. And my dad didn't. It wasn't until I reached eleven or twelve years old that I began to truly *understand* the very compelling reasons why my dad didn't seem to be there for me during my early years, and why he wasn't able to effectively communicate with me.

After I was born, my parents made an agreement that my mom would stay home with me and my dad would support us. As a result, he had to work six long days a week and many nights in order to enable my mom to raise me and for them to afford to give me a top-notch education. Additionally, my dad's father died when my dad was very young. So my dad essentially grew up without his father, whom he dearly loved. As a result, my dad had no fathering role model to emulate. And therefore, he just didn't know how to express his deep love for me.

Once I learned and was ready to *understand* and truly *appreciate* these realities, my poisonous energy charges triggered by my dad's seemingly non-loving behavior quickly dissipated. In the place of the rejection, hurt, and anger that I initially felt were feelings for my dad of forgiveness, sympathy (for his having lost his father at such an early age), compassion, appreciation, and pure, strong love. And as these feelings became more deeply embedded in my *Heart-of-Hearts*, almost all of the once-potent negative energy charges that were generated by my feelings of burning anger and profound hurt dissipated.

Additionally, it is also essential that you know and understand where *you* are coming from; because, if you can clearly see what is going on with and/or affecting you, then you are better able to:

1. be vigilant and proactive in not allowing a poisonous emotional state to dismantle (or continue to dismantle) your intellect;

2. be more focused on staying true to the things you want in and for your life; and

3. dissipate the potency of the emotion-generated energy charges that have flooded and/or are flooding you and your best judgment.

To illustrate this concept, I'd like to once again discuss the cases of Rebeccah and Danielle. However, before we go on to discuss them and their *paralyzing fears*, I would like to share some highly relevant research with regard to your dealing with the *fear* of "the unknown" and "change":

I am told that many years ago, an experiment was conducted with mice in a cage in order to learn how they would react to facing the unknown. As I understand it, one half of the cage floor on which all of the mice were standing was electrified. At various intervals, the feet of the mice were shocked, which made them jump and squeal in pain. After the mice received a series of shocks, the gate in the middle of the cage was opened so that the mice could go/flee to the other side of the cage, with the possibility that they could escape the shocks. The incredible result of this experiment was that *not one* mouse went over to the other side of the cage in order to avoid the shocks. For our purposes, at least two conclusions from this study can be drawn:

1. The fear of physical pain was preferred by or less daunting to the mice than was the fear of the unknown or the fear of change; and

2. The fear of the unknown seemed to be intellectually crippling to the mice, as it appears to have caused them not to think or act rationally; which may be one reason why not one mouse ventured over to the other side of the cage to see if "life" over there would be less painful.

In the case of Rebeccah, whom we discussed earlier, she was *frozen by fear* for years, as she was afraid to leave her poison-filled marriage to her demeaning, abusive, and sick husband, Brent. Much like the mice in the experiment cited above, Rebeccah was more comfortable existing/suffering in the constant psychological, emotional, and (occasional) physical pain of her marriage than leaving it for the unknown. However, when Rebeccah was (finally) able to *clearly see, understand,* and *appreciate* how the extremely high energy charges generated by her intense feelings of fear had time after time led her to make the horribly self-sabotaging life choice to remain with Brent, this became a *huge* step in breaking her destructive scripting.

Thereafter, when Rebeccah was able to identify and then pile on and amp up her *Golden* and *Truthful* energy charges, they so overwhelmed her now severely dissipated fear-based energy charges that she was *inevitably led* to leave Brent and their marriage *that day*!

As you may remember in the case of Danielle, the awesome, poisonous energy charges generated by the emotion of fear froze her, as well. She was faced with dwindling savings, a recession-damaged real-estate practice, and the responsibilities of being the sole means of support for her son and herself. What added to the intensity of her fear was her father's continually pushing her to find a secure corporate job in a field in which she had absolutely no interest. As a result, when Danielle contacted me, she was virtually paralyzed by her fear and thus unable to think, reason, choose, or act productively. In her case, it wasn't until Danielle identified, understood, and embraced what she most wanted and the person who she most wanted to be that she was able to significantly dissipate the high-voltage energy charges generated by her fear, and thereby think and reason far more clearly and logically at *Crunch Time!*. As we now know, Danielle wound up making the *Golden/Truthful* choices of seeking out and accepting a sales-representation position for a top-flight television-production company.

Reminder #5:

1. **One means to significantly dissipate the potency of poisonous energy charges is to understand and appreciate where you and relevant others are coming from.**

2. **By being understanding of others, you can grow to be respectful, compassionate, empathetic, and loving. All of these states can significantly diminish the intensity of your toxic energy charges.**

Reminder #6: Be *Consequence Cognizant*!

This calls for you to vividly visualize, in *the* harshest manner possible, the heinous and horrible consequences of your making a destructive or self-sabotaging life choice as a result of your being emotionally hijacked at *Crunch Time!*.

Once again, if John, the anchorman whom we discussed earlier, had been *Consequence Cognizant*, he could have identified the following potentially devastating consequences *before* he allegedly acted:

1. "The loss of the wonderful and cherished career that I currently enjoy;

2. the loss of my great, coveted, stimulating, prestigious job;

3. the loss of tremendous guaranteed income and the security it provides for me and my family;

4. being the direct cause of tremendous pain, angst, and embarrassment to my loving and wonderful wife and family;

5. living in ignominy for the rest of my life;

6. being accused of committing a felony;

7. being convicted of committing a felony;

8. enduring the tremendous, unhealthy stress of having to go
through all of these devastating consequences; and possibly
worst of all,

9. going to jail and serving an extended sentence there, and all
of the absolutely heinous consequences that would surely be
the result for me and my beautiful family."

As we previously discussed, if John had carefully considered all of
the horrible consequences of his emotion-filled act, the energy charges
from his once-awesome feelings of anger and betrayal could have been
significantly dissipated. As a result, he may well have opted to refrain
from allegedly acting in an extremely self-sabotaging manner.

Here's another illustration of being *Consequence Cognizant*:

Throughout each workday, I literally advise and counsel scores
of individuals. One component of this wonderful and spiritually
rewarding pursuit is that when I'm driving during my workday, I
receive many phone calls and texts. I'm a huge proponent of making every working second count by being as time-efficient as possible;
so, until recently, I would use my hands-free car phone to make and
return business calls and respond to texts whenever I stopped at traf-
fic lights. However, in my gut, I have always known that all of this
car-phone use—including glancing at and digesting my incoming
text messages while I'm driving—is distracting and can potentially
cause a fatal accident.

So, even though I dearly value the time I might save by

communicating with clients while I drive—by virtue of keeping all of the absolutely horrific and tragic potential consequences of my driving distracted in the forefront of my mind—I now choose to modify my behavior and drive more safely. Here are those consequences in detail:

1. SERIOUSLY INJURING OR KILLING A CHILD OR CHILDREN as they walk to and from the elementary school that I drive past each morning;

2. DESTROYING SOMEONE'S LIFE (and the lives of their loved ones) by seriously injuring or killing them;

3. DESTROYING MY LIFE because I caused a serious accident (perhaps one that could have been avoided) because I was distracted while driving; and

4. My DYING OR SUFFERING A CATASTROPHIC INJURY, such as brain damage or paralysis, because I wasn't focused on my driving.

Now, each time that I start my car, I think about and visualize the horrific consequences that could result from my not being an engaged driver. Because I am *Consequence Cognizant*, I no longer scroll down my car-computer phone book while driving, and I read and respond to text messages only *after* I have parked in a safe place. From my perspective, these are all very constructive life choices to make for the sake of preserving my well-being and that of others.

Reminder #6:

Be *Consequence Cognizant* at *Crunch Time!*.

Reminder #7: I could have included this *Reminder* as part of

Reminder #5; however, because *gratitude* and *appreciation* are such highly effective *Toxic-Energy-Charge Dissipaters*, I have chosen to make them part of a separate *Reminder*.

This *Reminder* calls for you to take full, deep breaths as you think, identify, and truly appreciate your blessings and make a *List* detailing them.

Three reasons to do this are:

1. You will dissipate the potency and intensity of your poisonous energy charges;

2. You are better able to keep the big picture of what you truly want in and for your life in perspective; and

3. You may well feel better after doing this if you are flooded with feelings of hurt, hopelessness, anger, rage, sadness, rejection, and/or disrespect.

Here's a sample *Blessing List*:

1. I'm healthy.

2. I have a beautiful family.

3. Overall, I have a great job/career.

4. I have my eyesight.

5. I have no major illnesses.

6. I have a pretty great life.

7. I play tennis and chess; as well as fish, ski, hike, paint, and write, all of which I love doing!

I often vividly recall a day, years ago, when I was walking around

Manhattan, and all sorts of things were irking me. And just as I was about to commence my internal pity party, I saw a blind, homeless man sleeping on the cold street. At his side was a cardboard sign that read, "Blind, homeless, and a starving U.S. Vet. Please help!"

As I absorbed this devastatingly sad reality, my heart ached terribly. I walked up to that gentleman and dropped some money into his cup, thinking, "*What could I possibly be unhappy or agitated about!?*"

As I left this seemingly unfortunate individual, I immediately forgot all of the truly insignificant stuff that had been upsetting me that day.

Reminder #7:

Acknowledging, appreciating, and truly feeling grateful for *your* blessings can put things in a better and brighter perspective and dissipate a great deal of the intensity of your poisonous, emotion-generated energy charges.

Reminder #8: Ask yourself: "What do I *truly* want to accomplish with this life choice?"; and "What kind of a person do I *truly* want to be?" As you may remember, when Philip asked himself these questions, his crystal-clear definitive values and *PETS* were:

1. "To be a person of God and do His work;

2. to be a good, loving father and husband;

3. to make life choices anger/rage-free so that they reflect what I truly want to accomplish;

4. to create, with Jan, a warm, loving family and home environment;

5. to do the opposite of what my grandfather and father did; that is, to treat my children with love and respect, and to make them feel loved and worthy, as opposed to subjecting them to violence, abuse, and intimidation;

6. to be rid of the burning anger and hatred that festers within me, and to live a life of peace; and

7. to continue to grow at my firm, so that I can continue to provide the financial stability for our family that my father never gave me or my mother and siblings."

Reminder #8:

Before making a life choice, always ask yourself and clearly *know* the answers to the following two questions: "What do I *truly* want to accomplish with this life choice?"; and "What kind of a person do I *truly* want to be?"

Reminder #9: Review what you prepared yourself to do at *Crunch Time!* during your *Prevent Offense* preparatory period:

> **9a.** Through the process of *event visualization*, recall the *specific* or *general* life choice that you prepared during your *Prevent Offense*. So, for example, when I was trying to lose weight, I recalled that my very *specific* response to being offered any form of fattening food would be an absolute "NO, THANK YOU!" Or, as we discussed earlier, an example of a more prepared flexible, *general* response is: "I won't go out

next week, because I'm behind on my schoolwork, *unless* someone *really* interesting asks me out. Then, and only then, will I make an exception."

9b. Mentally access the *Frame(s)* and *visual(s)* that you prepared when you anticipated having to make a particular life choice. To illustrate this, let's recall when I was using my analogue phone and I began experiencing shooting-pain headaches afterwards. After getting an MRI of my brain, I created *the* strongest *Frames* and *visuals* I could using the *PET* of being operated on for BRAIN CANCER as a result of holding my phone next to my ear. Thereafter, as soon as I had a choice to use my cell phone without the benefit of a headset to make or answer a call, or to wait until I had a headset, I'd immediately access my overpowering *Frame(s)* and *visual(s)* before making my life choice at *Crunch Time!*. As a direct result, I would delay the instant gratification of making or taking a call, which could/would jeopardize my health.

9c. Make sure that before you make a life choice, Your *PETS—Your Gold* and *Truth*—haven't changed since you last prepared or reviewed your *Prevent Offense*. As an illustration of this *Reminder*, let's once again study the case of Danielle. Initially, when Danielle and I first spoke, her purest *Gold* was:

1. to be able to support herself and her son Patrick;

2. to remain in her real-estate business; and

3. to avoid having to take a boring, corporate desk job,

such as working for the bank, as her father was pushing her to do.

However, during the time that I counseled Danielle, one very important piece of her *Gold* changed. As a result of some very effective self-exploratory work on Danielle's part, she unearthed that going back to the television industry as a salesperson would hold tremendous allure for her. And, after interviewing for a sales position at a top production company, she very happily accepted that offer and the job.

The point that is being illustrated here regarding Danielle's change in the valuation of her *Gold,* is that *Your Gold* and *Truth* can and often *will* change over time, and you must be aware of these changes in valuation before you craft your *Crunch Time! Frames* and *visuals.* This way, you will incorporate and utilize *only* the most current and most potent *PETS* (motivators) in your *Frisual.*

Additionally, it's also essential for you to discern the following: Are all of the variables that you anticipated during your *Prevent Offense* in connection with your life choice just as you anticipated?; have they changed?; or are they perhaps different? For example: You are a college student who is away at school. On Wednesday, you make the *ironclad, Prevent Offense* choice to not go out with anyone during the coming weekend—except Brad—so that you can study for exams. However, late Saturday afternoon, your parents and siblings pay you a surprise visit.

In this instance, a variable that you had no reason to anticipate has come into play and therefore must be taken into account before making any further life choice(s) as to how you will spend your Saturday evening and Sunday. This is an illustration of how a *specifically* anticipated life choice may need to be modified at *Crunch Time!* because of the introduction of new, important data.

Reminder #9:

Remember the choices you've prepared yourself to make at *Crunch Time!*. Additionally, recheck *Your Gold* and *Truth*, as well as discern whether there are any new variables that have come into play that you must now take into account as you make your choice(s).

Your *Crunch Time! Reminder Checklist*

Reminder #1: Strive for Intellectual Clarity ✓

Reminder #2: Remember and Acknowledge When You Made Similar, Destructive Life Choices In the Past ✓

Reminder #3: Identify Your Most Potent *PETS* ✓

Reminder #4: Bundle and Thereby Amp Up the Energy Charges That Will Lead You to Make *Golden/Truthful* Life Choices ✓

Reminder #5: Dissipate Potentially Toxic Energy Charges ✓

Reminder #6: Be *Consequence Cognizant* ✓

Reminder #7: Appreciate Your Blessings ✓

Reminder #8: Ask Yourself: "What Do I Really Want?" and "What Kind of a Person Do I Truly Want to Be?" ✓

Reminder #9: Remember What Choices You've Prepared Yourself to Make during Your *Prevent Offense*; Recheck *Your Gold* and *Truth*; and Discern Whether There Are Any New Variables That Need to Be Part of Your Life-Choice-Making Equation ✓

STEP 6

Make a *Golden/Truthful* Life Choice

$$\boxed{\text{Step 6}}$$

I t's now *Crunch Time!*, as you're faced with making a life choice. It's the moment that you've anticipated (*specifically* or *generally*) and effectively prepared for. It's literally your *Crunch Time!* to shine; to make a *Golden* and/or *Truthful* life choice; and to significantly raise the quality of your life, as well as your feelings of self-esteem and self-worth. And, as we've discussed, these good/great feelings will help to positively fill and nourish your *Heart-of-Hearts* and thereby *empower* you to make more and more *Golden/Truthful* life choices in the future, because you truly feel like you're *worth* making self-enhancing decisions for!

O.K. Let's take a closer look at *Step 6*:

1. You're faced with making a life choice;

2. You want to access your *Frame(s)* and *visual(s)* (your *Frisual[s]*), which have been carefully chosen and crafted for one very specific reason: They will inevitably motivate and lead you to make a *Golden/Truthful* life choice; and

3. You *will* with great fervor and passion seize this opportunity to *lift* your life, as well as your feelings of self-esteem and self-worth, by making a *Golden/Truthful* life choice at *Crunch Time!*.

O.K. Let's go over a *Golden/Truthful* life-choice illustration by virtue of revisiting the case of Ray, who was suffering from chronic acid reflux:

His doctor expressed strong concerns that if Ray didn't materially alter his diet and stop drinking alcohol, he would significantly increase his chances that he would contract throat and/or esophageal cancer—the same disease that Ray's father, grandfather, and uncle died of.

Here is the exceedingly high-voltage *Frame* that we developed so that Ray would stop drinking:

"Do I want the MOMENTARY pleasure/satisfaction of a drink and seriously increase my risk of GETTING CANCER!!!, and thereby reliving the HORRIBLE, PAINFUL, DEGRADING DEATH OF MY DAD, GRANDFATHER, AND UNCLE?; and even more importantly, do I want to risk NOT BEING WITH OR THERE FOR MY CHILDREN—ESPECIALLY LUANNE (his nine-year-old autistic daughter), WHO DESPARATELY NEEDS ME?;

Do I want to seriously risk putting MY CHILDREN and MOTHER THROUGH TREMENDOUS ANGUISH as they watch me DETERIORATE AND DIE from CANCER?; and

Do I want to be the cause—as a result of my weakness—of the ABSOLUTELY ABHORRENT reality of the INDESCRIBABLE PAIN that my mom would have to experience should she have to BURY HER ONLY CHILD?!!!;

OR...

Do I NOT DRINK and thereby give myself THE very best chance to BE THERE WITH THOSE I LOVE, TAKE CARE OF THEM—ESPECIALLY LITTLE LUANNE—and continue to LIVE!!! AN ACTIVE, HEALTHY LIFE; and NOT LET THOSE I LOVE DOWN?!"

Ray then chose his most motivating *visuals*—his family having to bury him and "Little Luanne" being left alone in the world, with *no one* to take care of and truly look after her.

Armed with his super-charged *Frame* and *visuals*, I am thrilled to say that except for two slips during the first six months, Ray has not had any alcohol for over two-and-a-half years! The severe irritation of his throat and esophagus is nearly gone. And, he remains both a loving, vital caretaker and son—his most potent *Gold* and *Truth*.

Your *Take-Away:*

At *Crunch Time!*, make a life choice that reflects and is consistent with your *Gold* and *Truth*.

I would now like to share a personal story illustrating how I went through my *Reminder List* and then *Step 6* at *Crunch Time!*:

I am blessed to own the very cutest Maltese puppy-girl named Peanut. She was given her name the moment that I first saw her and she came out of a room, ran up to lay lots of kisses on me, and compelled her owner to remark, "Look at *this* little peanut!" I instantly thought that with this puppy's adorable button-nose, "Peanut is the perfect name for her!" I absolutely love Peanut, and she, with her very sweet soul, loves everyone.

I live on a residential cul-
de-sac, where many of my
neighbors' children can normally play and walk their dogs
safely. However, one early evening, a neighbor, "Al," came
speeding up the street, turned
around the cul-de-sac as if he
were taking a curve at the Indy

500, and came to a screeching halt in front of his house.

Observing this incredibly dangerous and potentially life-threatening behavior, I walked up to Al and suggested that with all of the
children playing and walking their dogs on the block, he should drive
a good deal more slowly. During our brief interaction, Al seemed like
a very unhappy guy with a lot of pent-up anger. I could tell that my
suggestion didn't make him any happier. However, considering that
he had two young children of his own, who were always walking their
dogs and playing on our block, I thought that Al would have been a
bit more receptive to my suggestion.

Then, about a week or two later, after the sun had set and I was
walking Peanut, I saw Al's car, just a few yards away, once again speeding up the block. I began to yell for him to slow down. Al's windows
were closed, and he couldn't hear me. I then realized that he didn't
see little Peanut, who was a four-month-old, three-pound puppy. At
the very last second, I yanked Peanut away from his speeding tires.
It appeared as if Al missed running Peanut over by a mere inch or
two. Also, thankfully, my sudden yank of Peanut's leash didn't do any
damage to her neck or trachea.

I am not in any way a violent or a retaliatory individual; nor am I
subject to bouts of rage; but watching Al nearly kill Peanut made me
see red and got my blood boiling. I was seething!

The first thought that raced into my mind was to take one of the
baseball bats that Al's son had left on the street and smash the front

window of Al's car (now that Al had left the car). This way, maybe he'd think twice the next time that he decided to speed down our block! Just visualizing this made me smile (knowing I would never *really* do it), and it began to dissipate some of the high-voltage energy charges that were flooding me.

I then *immediately* went through my *Reminder List*:

#1. I must make a life choice with intellectual clarity. Therefore, I DO NOT want to make a choice or act when I'm overcome or under the influence of conflicting or potentially poisonous emotions.

#2. I must think about what happened the last few times I acted when I was angry and acknowledge that I almost always regretted my actions, as I later realized that there was a smarter and more effective way to have handled the situations and thereby secure better and more gratifying results.

#3. I must identify my big-picture *Gold*, which is to do all that I can to make sure that Al doesn't drive recklessly down our street again and endanger us all.

#4. I must amp up my positive energy charges, and I did. I identified my most potent *Gold* and *Truth*, as I thought about:

a. how much I want Peanut to be safe as she takes her walks down our block;

b. how much I want *everyone* to be safe;

c. how much I enjoy making life choices in a wise, evolved, and kind manner;

d. how much I value my freedom and life as I currently enjoy it, so that I wouldn't want to commit the crime of destroying Al's car;

e. how dumb and destructive it would be to lose my

temper with Al when *I'm* the one writing the book on mastering emotions!; and

f. how enraged I would be if Al, one day in the future, injured or killed little Peanut!

#5. I must dissipate my potentially toxic energy charges. I must also know myself and/or understand and appreciate where relevant others are coming from. I acknowledged in that knowing myself, I would feel as if I failed as an evolved person should I act poorly, and out of anger and/or rage. This would lead me to feel badly about myself. I know better than to let someone else's bad behavior cause me to act inappropriately.

Additionally, I did my best to try to understand where Al was "coming from," and to be compassionate and/or empathetic, and forgive him. I did this by acknowledging that I had already observed that Al seemed to be a very unhappy person. I was also sure that his reckless driving wasn't meant to hurt anyone. He probably just wasn't paying attention, as the energy charges from his obvious pent-up anger, frustration, and unhappiness were figuratively fueling him and his car.

#6. I must be *Consequence Cognizant*. And I was. I reasoned and visualized that if I actually did commit some physical act against Al's car:

a. I could go to jail;

b. I would risk losing the freedom and the life that I so very much enjoy and cherish;

c. I would be hugely disappointed in myself for how poorly I acted by letting my toxic energy charges dismantle my best judgment at *Crunch Time!*;

    d. I would lose all credibility regarding my ability to master my emotions and their energy charges; and

    e. I would profoundly embarrass myself, my family, and my clients.

#7. I must appreciate my blessings. I did this by taking a moment to remember and appreciate the wonderful life I have.

#8. I must identify and appreciate what I truly want and who I truly am and aspire to be. What I wanted was for Al to drive more carefully and safely. Who I aspire to be is a more thoughtful and evolved individual who continues to grow, and someone who chooses to deal with people and situations with intelligence, understanding, respect, and kindness—not with anger!

#9a. I must access my relevant *Prevent Offense* data, which I prepared for *Crunch Time!*. This included:

    a. *Never* make a life choice when I'm flooded with poisonous, emotion-generated energy charges; and

    b. Once I've calmed down, I must always strive to make the wisest, most evolved and enlightened choice of which I'm capable.

#9b. I must access the *Frame(s)* and *visual(s)* that I had prepared for the inevitable time when I would be faced with making a life choice while angry/enraged.

#9c. I must make sure that none of my *PETS* (my most important values) have changed. And they hadn't. I still wanted to act with clarity and precision and to handle things in a constructive and evolved way, so as to bring about a *Golden/Truthful* result for everyone. Additionally, I identified that no new variables that I hadn't anticipated entered into my life-choice equation. So, I was free to move forward with my *Frame* and *visual*.

Time to Make My Choice

I prepared a *Frame*:

> "Do I run up to Al in a rage; threaten him; yell at him; embarrass him and me; and thereby make him so defensive that he doesn't hear me?;
>
> OR...
>
> Do I calmly walk up to him and find an effective way to reach him, so that I can make sure that Peanut and others will be safe from his reckless driving?"

I then identified my *visual*:

> I pictured Al driving more carefully and sweet Peanut wagging her tail as she safely enjoys her walks down our street.

After going through the *Crunch Time! Reminder List*, I *consciously chose* to walk up to Al and try to have him *understand* and truly *appreciate* the potentially *horrific consequences* of his recklessly driving down our block. I chose to accomplish this by using an *emotional trigger* that I thought would strike a primal chord within him (his *PET*). I calmly said, "Al, you just missed hitting this cute little puppy of mine by a hair. Literally! It appears as if you don't care whom you might injure or kill as you speed down our block. But, I *know* that you *do* care! Tell me, how would *you* like it if someone unthinkingly sped down our block and KILLED ONE OF *YOUR* CHILDREN?" (I paused for a moment to let this horrible thought and image sink in.) "I know you're excited to get home and be with your beautiful family. But next time we all may not be so lucky by getting away with just a near miss."

After a quick moment, Al responded, "I'm so very sorry! It's Ken, right?"

I responded, "Yes," and shook Al's hand.

He then continued, "I'm *so* sorry. I just wasn't thinking. I was engrossed in a very ugly case that I'm litigating! You're *so* right! *Thanks* for this."

"My pleasure. Truly, Al. Have a great night, and please send my fondest regards to 'Kathy,' 'Dakota,' and 'Kirk!'"

"I will."

As a very direct result of my going through my *Reminder List*, effectively *Frisualing*, and (I believe) finding one of Al's most compelling *emotional triggers*, there were several positive outcomes:

1. I know that I *consciously* chose to act in a clear-thinking manner at *Crunch Time!*, which made me feel good;

2. In lieu of acting in anger and making Al act defensively, I was able to *effectively reason* and apparently hit home with Al, as he said that he was "truly sorry" about the speeding and explained that he "just wasn't thinking"; and

3. Al couldn't be more cordial whenever we now see each other, as he *very slowly* and *cautiously* drives down our block.

So lots of beneficial things can be attained if you think clearly and toxic-emotion-free at *Crunch Time!*.

Your Post-*Crunch Time!* Step

STEP 7

Review Your Life-Choice Process

Step 7

O.K., now that *Crunch Time!* is over and you've made your life choice, your last *Step* is to objectively and honestly review whether you are happy with the *Golden/Truthful* choice that you have made. If the answer is yes, it's important to acknowledge and celebrate it. However, if you feel that you didn't perform as well as you could have at *Crunch Time!*—and we *all* have times when we feel this way!—then it's time to identify what went wrong and get it right for the next *Crunch Time!*. So in essence, this *Step* of fixing any flaws or hiccups becomes your next *Prevent Offense* session.

O.K., let's focus on the case when you did in fact make a *Golden/Truthful* life choice at *Crunch Time!*.

Once you have successfully completed a *Frisual* and you've made a *Golden* and/or *Truthful* life choice, it's essential that you acknowledge, enjoy, and *feel* your wonderful accomplishment(s).

This is a key process for you, because, when you effectively *Frisual*, master your emotions and their energy charges, and then make a *Golden/Truthful* life choice, it is incredibly *empowering*. To take your fate into your very capable hands, and choice by choice create the life you've dreamed about, is *empowering*. To *own* your choices and your destiny is *empowering*. To *truly know* that you can consistently accomplish all of this is *empowering*! And all of these high-self-esteem building feelings generate supremely powerful positive energy charges that you can store in your *Heart-of-Hearts*. As a result, when you are faced with making future life choices and you *Frisual*, you can draw upon these tremendously positive, stored energy charges in order to combine them with and amp up the ones derived from *Your Gold* and *Your Truth*; the effect is a further decimation of the competing energy charges generated from potentially poisonous emotions.

So, in order for you to keep filling your *Heart-of-Hearts* with your most potent, positive energy charges, here are some highly beneficial post-*Golden/Truthful* life-choice acts:

1. *Acknowledge* the fact that you *Framed* and *visualized* (*Frisualed*) the choice before you in such an effective manner that you were inevitably led to make a life choice that enabled you to attain *Your Gold* and/or brought you closer to living *Your Truth*. All wonderful and fulfilling things that should exhilarate you and make you very proud!;

2. *Celebrate and savor a Frisual* well executed and a life choice well thought-out and made, free from the sabotaging-emotion-generated energy charges that might normally have clouded or derailed your best judgment; and

3. *Feel and enjoy* your triumph and your POWER! The more you feel and enjoy your accomplishments, the more they will energize and motivate you to make many, many more *Golden/Truthful* life choices in the future. This is so because you've seen and enjoyed the extremely beneficial results of your life-choice-making, and you feel in your

Heart-of-Hearts that you and your bright future are worth making *Golden/Truthful* life choices for.

Your *Take-Away:*

When you acknowledge, celebrate, and *feel* that you have made a *Golden* and *Truthful* life choice, the result is that you generate highly positive feelings of empowerment. These feelings will be stored in your *Heart-of-Hearts.* As a result, when you next *Frisual,* you can tap into these strong, positive feelings to help amp up your positive energy charges in order to overpower your poisonous ones.

Now let's discuss how to correct your *Crunch Time!* stumbles, so as to improve and enhance your future *Crunch Time!* life-choice-making experiences.

The Stumble

When performing *The 7 Steps of Emotion Mastery,* it is essential that you never lose sight of the following Core Concept:

> As human beings, we have the abilities to think, value, reason, learn, grow, evolve, and attain tremendous things and heights. But, being human, we will also make mistakes, stumble, and suffer setbacks. Learning to constructively pick yourself up after stumbles is part of everyone's growth process.

The thought for you to keep in mind here is this: One or two rain-drops do not a flood make; a couple of snowflakes do not a blizzard make; a few pebbles do not an avalanche make; and one or two mistakes or stumbles do not generally a catastrophe or a failure make! And, in almost all cases, there is always tomorrow.

No matter how evolved, smart, and/or talented we are, we will *never* do everything perfectly, every time! Huge success is attained by doing the "right" things most of the time; and as we have already discussed, it is hugely important to *Come Up BIG!* when your most cherished *Gold* and your purest *Truth* are at stake.

In connection with stumbles, when I first started to *Frisual*, no matter how very much I craved my dad's love and approval, I would still occasionally stumble and suffer a setback by eating cake, cookies, and/or candy in order to assuage my poisonous feelings and needs. But, the key is that these occurrences became more and more infrequent so that they weren't devastating slips or didn't become habitual. And as I began to lose more and more weight, my empowering energy charges in my *Heart-of-Hearts* became stronger and stronger. So, my very occasional stumbles didn't have a major impact on my weight-loss efforts, my confidence to effect positive change in my life, or the huge positive energy charges that I channeled into my *Frisuals*.

By the by, as I've now been slim for many decades, I can every once in a while splurge with no regrets. But *I'm* in total control! And, if I do see that I've gained some weight or my pants feel a little tight, I become a much more proactive *Frisualer*—and I quickly drop the weight.

So, always be equipped with the following profound insight and understanding:

> "O.K. If I'm going to strive to attain my *Gold*, along my journey, I *will* have some missteps. This is a given, as *everyone has stumbles*! The key is to be armed with the rock-solid emotion-mastery foundation provided in this book, along with the ability to implement its *Steps*, thinking, and strategies. If you are, the mistakes

and stumbles will occur far less frequently, and your triumphs will come far more often and easily."

Just stay true to your purest, most potent *Gold* and *Truth*, and the missteps won't mean much of anything or be very significant.

Correction Day

As we just discussed, you won't be able to make every life choice to your ideal specifications. There will be occasional flaws in your *Prevent Offense* preparation, your *Frisual*, or your follow-through, in that you won't always take actions that are consistent with your ideal *Golden/Truthful* life choices. As a result, at some point after their execution, it will be time to reflect upon and fix what might have gone wrong or what you could have done better. The perfect time to do this is when you are able to reflect and clearly see—poisonous-emotion-generated, energy-charge free—what truly transpired. This way, you're dealing with the honest, unobstructed truth.

Years ago, I was listening to ESPN Radio when I heard a University of Southern California football player talk about the Monday following the team's Saturday game. That player basically said that Monday was *Correction Day* for the team. This meant that the players and the coaching staff would carefully and non-defensively study the videotapes from Saturday's game. Their goals were to:

1. identify and fix their flaws, missteps, or the things that they could improve upon, so that they would be better equipped to secure sweet victories in their upcoming games; and

2. identify the things that they did well—and see if they could execute them even better—so that they could continue to capitalize on these skills and assets in the future.

As important as it is for you to acknowledge, celebrate, savor, enjoy, and *feel* your *Frisual* and life-choice victories so that you are able to channel these awesome energy charges into your *Heart-of-Hearts* and later tap into this supremely potent reservoir of positive energy, it is equally as important to honestly and non-defensively identify and acknowledge how you could have done things (even) better or more skillfully so that you don't make the same preparatory or *Crunch Time!* missteps again when you're presented with your next life choice.

Always remember that *everyone* occasionally stumbles when endeavoring to master their emotions. The key, when you do make a mistake or you could have done something better, is to:

1. honestly and non-defensively identify the misstep;

2. visualize it;

3. figure out *how* to be more effective as you prepare your next *Prevent Offense* or *Frisuals* and/or make your future *Golden/ Truthful* life choices; and

4. try not to repeat the same misstep in the future.

Your *Take-Aways:*

1. As a human being, you will have missteps, stumbles, and setbacks. Don't be concerned. We all have them! Just keep following and practicing the *Steps* and strategies of *Your Killer Emotions*.

2. It is essential for you to continually review and improve upon any missteps that you have made. This way, the next time that you *Frisual*, you will be better prepared and equipped to secure and enjoy a more beneficial and gratifying result.

PART 3

The Finishing Touches

Chapter 1

"*PET* Care" — The Importance of Continually Checking Your *PET* Potency

Throughout your life, it is essential to continue to regularly mine and accurately (re)prioritize *Your Gold* and *Your Truth*—that is, to assess whether what you identified at some earlier time as your most dearly held *Gold* and/or *Truth* still qualifies as such. Or, has there possibly been a change in your *valuation* of some goal, dream, or desire?

You must also ask yourself, "Has the passage of time or the gaining of some new information or insight made a certain goal more or less important to me, and therefore more or less of a priority for me than it was before?" For example, earlier we discussed how College Student A had made the choice on Wednesday to take the upcoming weekend to study, opting not to go out with *anyone*. However, when Student A's parents and siblings made a surprise visit on Saturday afternoon, studying that evening took a backseat to (or was deemed to be of lesser value than) spending the evening with her family, whom she *greatly* missed.

The valuation of your current emotion-generated energy charges is of crucial import because, as we have discussed, the more you value your *Gold*, the higher its energy charge is for you. Remember, your goal when you *Frisual*™ is to always amp up your *Frisual* with as many potent energy charges as possible; your bundle of *Golden/Truthful* life-choice-evoking energy charges ALWAYS needs to overpower your potentially destructive and sabotaging energy charges, thereby allowing you to think clearly and logically when you make your life choices. This is how you will *attain* your *Gold* and *Truth*. Additionally, by keeping *Your Gold* and *Truth* current, you can SUSTAIN your success . . . , which is incredibly important!

Here's an illustration of this by way of a story:

A few years ago, I was contacted by one of the country's most well known weight-loss companies (e.g., Weight Watchers, Jenny Craig, Nutri-Systems). An executive from this company explained to me that in the great majority of cases when an individual signs up with the company to lose weight, the client does so because, in essence, some specific person or event (or potential event) in that client's life was triggering this decision.

This catalyzing event might be a New Year's resolution (e.g., "New Year, new me!"); a new love interest; the spring and summer bikini/swimsuit season's (impending) arrival; an upcoming wedding; a new job; or an approaching vacation. This executive then shared the profound problem for his company: "We get a slew of new signups, but then the drop-off rate after four or five weeks is tremendous." He continued by telling me, "The individuals who become members are *initially* motivated, for whatever their reason is, to begin losing weight, but when they lose that *initial motivation*—which often happens very quickly—we never hear from them again. There's no *staying power*." This executive wanted my counsel and help in connection with how his company could enable its clients to *sustain their motivation over time* to want to lose weight.

Although I didn't move forward with that company, my analysis regarding this huge drop-out problem is that everyone who makes the life choice to sign up and begin dieting so that he or she can lose weight does so because of the energy charge(s) generated from a certain piece or pieces of his or her *Gold* (e.g., wanting to fit into a bikini or swimsuit because the appropriate season is here).

The two relevant issues for us to explore here are as follows:

1. Are the energy charges generated by the *Gold* that motivated the individuals to sign up and begin dieting potent enough to empower them to *sustain* this positive life-choice-making (dieting) over a prolonged period of time?; and

2. Once the initial motivating event or person *goes away* or isn't as compelling as it once was, does the *Golden* energy wattage that remains have enough "juice" to overpower the competing and conflicting energy charges of potentially poisonous and sabotaging emotions that could ultimately lead the person to regain the weight?

I believe that the answer to question 1 is: "It depends upon the potency of the energy charges, but probably not." The answer to question 2, in a great majority of cases, is simply: "No!" Once the initial motivating factor goes away or is less compelling, almost all weight-loss-seeking clients run out of steam. As a direct result, these clients stop dieting and gain all of their weight back, and these companies lose all of these clients.

The very good news for you is that through *The 7 Steps of Emotion Mastery*, you have taken care of both of these potential problems because:

1. When you make a life choice to do something (such as lose weight; become more punctual; stop drinking/smoking, or

the like), you are fueled by your very strongest, most compelling energy charges, which are generated by your most cherished *Gold* and *Truth*. So, because your initial triggering energy charges are *so very strong*, you are far more likely to remain on the life-enhancing course; and, even more importantly,

2. You are committed to *regularly* mining and re-prioritizing your *Gold*, so that when one piece of *Gold* is no longer as important, compelling, or desirable as it once was—which therefore diminishes the potency of its available energy charge—*you replace it with another, equally or more valuable piece of Gold*, whose energy charge is as high or higher than the one it replaced. As a result, *you continue* to be fueled and catalyzed to act by the supremely motivating forces of your *PETS*, which generate *the* very highest-voltage energy charges; these *PETS* motivate and lead you to *continue* to make *Golden/Truthful* life choices, and thereafter act consistently with them! Therefore, staying on a *Golden/Truthful* course (such as a diet or any program) for the long term is far easier and much more likely.

Using my weight-loss story as an illustration of the above, as soon as my motivating energy-charged *Gold* became less potent because:

1. I began to feel my dad's love, approval, and respect;

2. I began to wear all of the cool, tapered clothes that I desired; and

3. I realized that even though I was slim, I was not going to be perceived romantically by Dale,

I was able to find *other Gold* to either supplement these energy charges or replace them. Some of my new pieces of *Gold* were:

1. I want to stay thin and fit in order to become the very best Extreme Tennis player of which I am capable;

2. I want to stay thin and fit because I aspire to be a great tennis player;

3. I want to stay thin and fit because I love the romantic attention that I am now receiving from (other) girls;

4. I love looking good and feeling great about myself!;

5. I love staying thin and fit because I want to enjoy a long, healthy, and vital life—like my dad;

6. I never want to be the insecure "FAT SLOB" that I was before. Never! Never! NEVER again!; and

7. As I finish writing this book, I need to stay thin in order to illustrate how effective *The 7 Steps of Emotion Mastery* are!

So, if you want to continue throughout the rest of your life to make *Golden/Truthful* life choices and thereafter act consistently with them, it is crucial for you to *continually* mine and (re)evaluate *Your Gold*, so as to channel *only* your most (current) potent *Gold* and *Truth* into your *Frisuals*.

Your *Take-Away:*

Keep mining *Your Gold* and *Truth*, and, if necessary, keep amending your *Lists*. This way, you will *always* be tapping into, harnessing, and channeling your highest-voltage *Gold* and *Truth* into your *Frisuals*. By doing this, you can SUSTAIN your *Golden* and *Truthful* life-choice-making—in every area—throughout your life!

Chapter 2

Pitfalls to Avoid at *Crunch Time!*

Now that you have read and absorbed *The 7 Steps of Emotion Mastery*, we will assume that you are well on your way to being able to think, reason, and evaluate with crystal clarity at *Crunch Time!*.

As a result, it's time to discuss some things that you *do not* want to do at *Crunch Time!* that can lead you to make self-destructive life choices in spite of all the work that you've put in.

Pitfall #1: Do Not Opt for an Inappropriate Quick Fix: Failure to Use Appropriate Discipline and Delayed Gratification When They Are Called for

Dr. M. Scott Peck, in *A Road Less Traveled*, astutely writes, "Discipline is the basic set of tools we require to solve life's problems. Without discipline, we can solve nothing!"[F]

As you have seen throughout *Your Killer Emotions*, the appropriate use of disciplined thinking and behavior will be one of your great-est allies as you grow to master your emotions and attain what you truly want. Conversely, the lack of discipline can be one of your big-gest downfalls. As a society, we all face the challenge of wanting and requiring immediate gratification. For example, how often do we hear in the most positive context, "We want what we want, and we want it NOW!"? Many of us have become attention-impaired, and we therefore seek quick, easy, and painless fixes, remedies, solutions, and payoffs—even if the quality of the satisfaction that we derive from such remedies, solutions, and payoffs is compromised, diluted, hollow, and short-lived. We are no longer taught that it is often wise to value investing our time and energy in something that may require longer periods of maturation; some hard, focused work; and delayed gratification. In essence, we're not taught or reinforced by our society to learn and practice the art of being disciplined.

But here's the profound, conflicting problem regarding this sorry state of affairs: Today, more than ever, you're constantly bombarded in all sorts of ways with messages suggesting that seeking and attain-ing immediate gratification or a quick fix to a problem is O.K., or even desirable. Additionally, when you are in the midst of making important life choices and you are flooded with potentially poison-ous emotions such as hurt, anger, sadness, rage, neediness, hopeless-ness, resentment, jealousy, self-loathing, insecurity, and/or (sexual) urges, it very often appears (and is) far easier to opt for the choice that will quickly make you feel good or even merely "better" as you assuage the pain, fill the void, calm the "bad" feeling, or satisfy the urge *at the time, for the moment.*

As a result, many times the energy charges from these poten-tially poisonous, intense emotions and urges will lead you to make life choices that are in direct conflict with what you know, in your best-reasoned judgment, to be right and beneficial for you *in the long term.* Therefore, these shortsighted choices, which are fueled by your potentially self-destructive emotions and their energy charges, will derail and/or destroy your opportunities to attain *Your Gold* and live *Your Truth*. And later, upon clear reflection, you will realize that you have let yourself down—big-time—by making a poor or self-destructive choice yet again. This spirit- and confidence-deflating experience and realization will (once again), in all likelihood, lower your self-esteem and confidence and foster deep and strong feelings within you of negative inevitability/resignation/hopelessness. These feelings in turn will lead you to make more self-destructive choices in the future because you lack the highly motivating feeling of high self-worth and the core confidence to aspire to better things.

As a *Golden/Truthful* life-choice maker, the appropriate use of discipline and delayed gratification, when used in concert with *The 7 Steps*, will enable you to combat the emotions and urges that, in the past, have compelled you to settle for a self-sabotaging and self-esteem-deflating quick fix.

Pitfall #2: Do Not Make Important Life Choices When You're Tired: The Importance of Adequate Rest and Being Free from Intellect-Dulling Influences

It has been said that you "don't [want to] go to a grocery store when you're hungry, [as] you'll make bad decisions." The very insightful message for us here is that you shouldn't put yourself in a position to make a life choice when your intellectual clarity can be hijacked by overpowering emotions or urges. Conversely, whenever you are preparing to make an important life choice, it is essential to put yourself in the best position possible to make that choice free from intellect-dulling and intellect-nullifying influences.

The world's most proficient performers, such as Olympians or the very top professional athletes, know that they need to be well rested, as well as physically, mentally, and emotionally fresh and in top shape when they compete. They must perform their tasks with *clarity* and *precision*, so that they put themselves in the very best position to *Come Up BIG!* at *Crunch Time!*, when it truly counts.

When you make your life choices, you, too, need to *Come Up BIG!* at *Crunch Time!* so that you can consistently attain *Your Gold* and live *Your Truth*. What this means is that when you are making important choices, you must consistently bring your intellectual and emotional "A game" to the table. One way to consistently do this is to be intellectually and emotionally clear and sharp. This requires that you be *well rested and free from the judgment and intellect-dulling influences of lack of sleep, drugs and alcohol, caffeine, and stress.*

LACK OF SLEEP

It is essential when making important life choices that you can think, reason, and value clearly. Being well rested, fresh, and on top of your intellectual game can most certainly help you accomplish this. I know from personal experience, and from the experiences of numerous others, that we've all been emotionally hijacked and made self-destructive decisions when we were tired. So, as best you can, make your life choices when you are well rested, fresh, and in control of your emotions. On the other hand, do your very best NOT to make important life choices when you're tired and feel like the weight of everything and everyone is upon you. What you want is intellectual clarity—not intellectual nullification caused by your being overpowered by potentially poisonous energy charges.

DRUGS AND ALCOHOL

As discussed above, you want to make choices with crystal intellectual clarity. You want to be in control and deal with real, pure data. Therefore, do not make life choices under the influence of alcohol or any recreational or medicinal drug! This is absolute, pure common sense!

CAFFEINE

If you have anger-management challenges, do not make life choices when you are hopped-up on caffeine.

STRESS

A few days before Christmas, I was in an elevator with a prominent criminal attorney. During our conversation, he mentioned that he is always busiest during Christmas, New Year's, birthdays, and other times when individuals are under more stress than usual. He said that generally, crimes of passion, sexual abuse, and battery rise when people are under stress. He warned, "When people are stressed-out, they make their absolute *worst* choices!"

Always remember that stress can block or dismantle your reasoning processes and the use of your best judgment. It can also amp up the voltage of the energy charges generated by your potentially poisonous emotions. Therefore, it is essential for you to do your very best not to make important life choices when you are under increased or high stress.

Pitfall #3: Do Not Put Yourself in a Position to Fail

This book is all about stacking the deck heavily in your favor with respect to making *Golden/Truthful* life choices. One way to accomplish this is not to put yourself in a position that will or may well lead you to make a self-destructive life choice. What this means is that you do not want to do something or refrain from doing something that will allow the energy charges from your sabotaging emotions to override and derail your best-reasoned judgment at *Crunch Time!*.

As we discussed earlier, you shouldn't go into a grocery store when you're famished and trying to lose weight. Why? Because you significantly increase the chances that you will opt for the quick fix of having some cookies or a pastry and go off your diet. Another, far more serious illustration of this dynamic occurred in the Kobe Bryant, Eagle, Colorado incident when Kobe was charged with criminal sexual assault. The lesson in this instance is: If you're a married man and you don't want to be unfaithful to your wife and/or you don't want to put your career, image, livelihood, and freedom in harm's way, you don't invite a woman whom you're sexually attracted to into your hotel room. Because if you do, you significantly increase the percentages that the awesome power of the energy charges generated by your sexual urge will overpower and thereby dismantle your sound, long-term judgment at *Crunch Time!* and lead you to make a potentially disastrous life choice.

As they say, if you don't want to get burned, don't play with fire. As a *Golden/Truthful* life-choice maker who wants to be a life winner, don't even carry any matches or other means to start a life-destructive fire. Once again, this is common sense!

Your *Take-Aways:*

1. At *Crunch Time!*, you want to think with crystal clarity and make your life choices with great thought, right-on perception and intuition, and precision.

2. Being disciplined and being able to delay gratification are skills that are essential for you to develop and utilize so that you can make life choices, time after time, that reflect your purest *Gold* and *Truth*.

3. When you make your life choices, you must be very careful to ensure that your intellect and reasoning processes aren't dimmed or dismantled by lack of sleep, or because you are under the potentially sabotaging influences of alcohol, drugs, or stress. If you are subject to any of the aforementioned intellect-dimming influences, you often become far more vulnerable to being emotionally flooded and derailed by poisonous energy charges at *Crunch Time!*. As a result, you are far more likely to make self-destructive and self-sabotaging, quick-fix life choices.

4. Do not put yourself in positions that significantly increase the percentages that the energy charges from your sabotaging emotions will overpower, and thereby nullify, your best judgment.

Chapter 3

Develop Your *Quick Frames*™ and *Quick Pics*

et's go back for a moment to Pavlov's stimulus-response study. If you remember, with repetition, the dog in Pavlov's experiment began to automatically or reflexively salivate, even without the stimulus of the meat being present. So, too, when you continue to successfully make more and more *Golden/Truthful* life choices, the past positive results, coupled with the ever-growing huge, positive-emotion-generated energy charges that are stored in your *Heart-of-Hearts*, may well lead you to automatically or reflexively make *Golden/Truthful* life choices in the future without your having to engage in a full set of *Prevent Offense* preparatory *Steps* or a full *Frisual*. At some point, you may only need a *Quick Frame*™ and/or a *Quick Pic* to bring about the desired result, which is your *Golden/Truthful* life choice.

Let me illustrate. After my having made a series of triumphant life choices to refrain from eating anything fattening, I lost weight, and:

1. I became a much better athlete, which allowed me to bond

with my dad athletically. This enabled me to attain my purest *Gold* of attaining and feeling my dad's love, approval, and respect;

2. I had girls to whom I was attracted view me romantically (as opposed to platonically) because I looked better, I was more fun to be around, and I felt better about myself and was more confident;

3. I attained significant success in both tennis and Extreme Tennis;

4. I experienced tremendously high-voltage, empowering feelings of high self-esteem because, through making my *Golden/Truthful* life choices, I was able to take positive ownership of and create a life that I could feel great about; and

5. I tangibly felt and enjoyed the very sweet life-choice-making fruits that were the direct result of my effective implementation of *The 7 Steps of Emotion Mastery.*

Over time, all of these positive occurrences energized and empowered me to *automatically* make self-enhancing dietary and healthy life choices without my having to spend extensive time on my *Prevent Offenses* and *Frisuals*. Essentially, making these *Golden/Truthful* life choices became almost *reflexive.* Little or no thought or effort on my part was needed, as all of the potentially conflicting and poisonous emotional energies that had once had such an impactful influence no longer held any real juice. At some point, these once poisonous emotions and their energy charges were so devastatingly overpowered and overridden by my new, far stronger combination of *PET* energy charges that their pull barely, if at all, existed. However, for the times when there was an energy-charge conflict, and I didn't want to take a misstep, I had my *Quick Frames* and *Quick Pics* at the ready.

Because I have *Frisualed* for decades and continue to regularly mine my *Gold* and *Truth*, I am very well aware of the *Frames* and *visuals* that most effectively push my emotional buttons. So, for example, whenever I feel like eating something fattening, and I don't think that it's the time or place to go off my diet, I do a *Quick Frame*, which is my shorthand. I just say to myself, "FAT SLOB" or "FAT PIG"—which is shorthand for, "Do I once again want to be that 'FAT SLOB/FAT PIG' whom I hated and develop a potbelly and stomach tires like all those men I see who have let themselves go?" And then I instantaneously visualize myself sitting on a beach counting the disgusting rolls of fat around my stomach, as I did when I was a boy. So, my *Quick Frame* ("FAT SLOB!") and my *Quick Pic* ("TIRE BOY!") are enough to put me back in line so that I can continue to make *Golden/Truthful* dietary life choices.

Another illustration of this cognitive and visual shorthand can be seen in my decision to no longer hold my cell phone directly up to my ear. After repeatedly relying on my *Frisual* to stop me from even thinking about using a cell phone without a headset or the use of the speaker function, eventually I just needed to use the following *Quick Frame* and *Quick Pic*, respectively:

"Do I want BRAIN CANCER and BRAIN SUR-GERY?"

I then visualized myself being wheeled into the operating room for BRAIN-CANCER SURGERY.

Eventually, I only needed a *Quick Frame* of two words: "BRAIN CANCER." They were more than enough!

You've heard of pocket-sized stain-remover sticks (such as Tide To Go™), which are to be used when you are on the go. Well, *Quick Frames* and *Quick Pics* are your *Frisuals* on the go. *Quick Frames* and *Quick Pics* can be effectively used once you have the required amount of positive, super-high-voltage emotional-energy charges and the requisite number of life-choice-making victories in the given area stored in your *Heart-of-Hearts*. *Quick Frames* and *Quick Pics* can act as your most effective, on-the-spot, life-choice-making allies...especially for snap-second decisions.

The "F" Word

Years ago, "Tom" asked for my help regarding some temper problems that he had not been able to overcome. One challenge was that he often blurted out the "F" word or the "M-F" words at inappropriate times. In years past, his outbursts had embarrassed him. At work, he had been written up and reprimanded for his use of foul language. However, none of this compelled him to remedy the problem.

But then he met "Lisa," whom he was head-over-heels about. (His most potent *Gold*.) After a few dates, Tom learned that the recently divorced Lisa *abhorred* crude language or behavior. (Oh, "F!") He also surmised that if Lisa hated foul language, she would probably leave him in a hot second if he used any inappropriate "cuss words" in front of her four-, six-, and nine-year-old sons. So Tom was scared to death that he would let his emotions or reflexive responses overtake him and that he'd drop the "F" bomb in front of Lisa, or, perish the thought and *visual*, in front of her kids.

In this case, Tom's purest *Gold* was easy to identify: to develop a loving, committed, long-term relationship with Lisa, and to do everything possible "not to 'F' it up" by using the "F" word around Lisa or her children.

The first step in our *Choreography* was to develop our most effective *Prevent Offense*, during which we identified the fact that Tom has had a long-running problem regarding his now reflexive "crude" outbursts, and that he had to put a quick, definitive end to this behavior.

Tom then anticipated and visualized all of the foreseeable instances in the future when he might blurt out the "F" word. We strategized as to what words he could say as cathartic substitutes for the term. Trust me, this was a very colorful discussion! We concluded that even saying "Friggin'" would be too crude for Lisa and/or the kiddies. As a result, we eventually decided that initially, he would use the following two terms for *cathartic satisfaction*: "Façonnable" (the manufacturer of the shirt I was wearing) for the "F" word; and "mother-father" for the "M-F" term. However, our ultimate goal was to eventually have Tom eliminate the need to use any of these expletive substitutes to express his frustration and/or anger.

We then did our *Frisual*. Tom *Framed* the issue before him as follows: "Do I want to stop and think *before* I express my frustration or anger and not say *anything* that might cause me to LOSE THE WOMAN—LISA—I'M SO VERY MUCH IN LOVE WITH; OR, do I continue, as I have, to be TOTALLY UNDISCIPLINED in how I express myself, and thereby run the tremendous risk that I WILL LOSE LISA FOREVER!, and as a direct result, my life will go back to being the same MISERABLE, LONELY, UNHAPPY EXISTENCE it was before?"

The easy, inevitable answer for Tom was: "I *cannot ever* use questionable language in front of Lisa or her children!"

We then did a *visual* of the likely abhorrent scenario of Tom reacting to an anger-, frustration-, or hurt-evoking event, and his unthinkingly blurting out an obscenity; with the horrific result that Lisa runs—not walks—out of his life *forever*! This image made Tom visibly cringe. In fact, this *visual* affected Tom so profoundly that during our next conversation, Tom told me that he had decided to quit using all questionable or cathartic substitute language, cold turkey! They say that "love conquers all." In Tom's case, his most potent *Gold* absolutely did! His deep love for Lisa, and his tremendous optimism regarding the future that they could enjoy together (his most potent *PETS*), yielded such supremely powerful energy charges that except for one, nipped-in-the-bud near-slip, Tom has been able to eliminate *all* foul language from his repertoire for over six months. For the last four months of this period, whenever Tom felt an emotion coming on that had even the slightest potential to elicit a language misstep, he employed the following *Quick Frame* and *Quick Pics*:

> The *Quick Frame*: "CAN'T LOSE LISA!"

> The *Quick Pics*: vividly visualizing (1) Lisa's beautiful, bright, warm smile; and (2) Lisa leaving him *forever* because he said something crude in front of her or her children.

Great work, Tom!
Here's one final illustration:

My dear, longtime friend, "Hank," was told by his doctor that if he didn't significantly change and improve his diet and lose a substantial amount of weight, he would very likely contract diabetes...a disease that his father died from at a very early age.

After consulting with me and developing his *Frames* and *visuals*, we soon thereafter crafted his *Quick Pic*—a lovely picture of his beautiful family standing together—and his *Quick Frame*: "DEADLY! DIABETES."

Equipped with these impactful tools, within the first six weeks of our working together, Hank lost over twenty pounds. After thanking me for my help in enabling him to accomplish this, he said that he would *never* put his life in jeopardy again!

In response to Hank's confident declaration, I thought to myself, "*This time*, I truly expect that he will stay on his heartfelt dietary course."

I say, "This time," because throughout the many years that I've known Hank, he, like many other well-intentioned individuals, would lose a great deal of weight, hit an emotional pothole weeks later, and gain all of the weight back—and then some. However, *this* time *will* indeed be different, because Hank will be motivated by his very strongest *PETS*—his fervent desire to be alive for the sake of his family and to not die from diabetes, as his dad did.

But, if he does happen to go off his diet for any significant period of time because his *Frames* and *visuals*—and his *Quick Frames* and *Quick Pics*—lose some of their highly potent juice, he/we will add new pieces of *Gold* and *Truth* to replace the ones that no longer generate the very strongest energy charges. This way, Hank can hopefully enjoy a long, healthy, diabetes-free life as a direct result of his *consistently* making lifelong *Golden* and *Truthful* dietary choices.

Your *Take-Away:*

Your *Quick Frames* and *Quick Pics* are your *Frame* and *visual* shorthand. In time, *Quick Frames* and *Quick Pics* can be as highly energy-charged and effective as your original full *Frames* and *visuals* in inevitably leading you to make *Golden* and *Truthful* life choices.

Chapter 4

A Final Thought and Wish

We have discussed that it is not enough to *know* what you want in and for your life. No matter how smart and talented you are, you must *also* be in control of your emotions, feelings, impulses, compulsions, and urges—and their energy charges—when you make your life choices and thereafter act.

You now have the *7 Steps*, the thought processes, the strategies, and the skills with which to master your emotions and the ability to use—as your allies—the awesome energy charges generated by your purest, and therefore your most potent, *Gold* and *Truth*. You are now ready, time after time, to overpower and thereby nullify the energy charges generated by your potentially poisonous emotions. This will enable and empower you to make life choices and take actions that are based upon and reflect your most well thought-out best judgment. As a result, you will attain your *Gold* and come ever closer to living *Your Truth*.

You can now take empowering and exhilarating OWNERSHIP of your life choices and actions, and create the life of which you've always dreamed!

Picture your life starting today as a big, clean, fresh white canvas—with you thoroughly equipped to be THE most wonderfully skilled and gifted painter. So be a Picasso or a Monet, and paint beautiful, empowered pictures of *your* life and that of others! BE A LIFE-CHOICE-MAKING ROCK STAR!

I'm incredibly excited for you!

HERE'S TO YOUR BRAND-NEW, TOXIC-EMOTION-FREE BEGINNING!

Some Suggestions for Your Therapist or Counselor Regarding *Extra-Strength, Toxic-Energy-Charge Dissipation*™ and *Destructive, Generational, Emotion-Triggered Scripting*

B eing an effective, insightful, and intuitive therapist or counselor when it comes to *Toxic-Energy-Charge Dissipation* is an art. Therefore, I respectfully would like to provide some suggested guidelines for whomever you choose as your therapist or counselor in helping you to dissipate the high-voltage energy charges triggered by your *Destructive, Emotion-Generated Scripting*, generational or otherwise.

Here is a set of 8 steps that have been highly effective for me in helping those individuals whom I've counseled:

Step 1. Ask your client about the backgrounds of his or her immediate family members, as well as about those of any relevant extended family members. Look for all kinds of stories and nuggets of information about the families, funny or otherwise.

Step 2. Pay special attention to any *repeated* patterns or similarities in the described incidents and behaviors of forbears, as well as to those of immediate family members.

Step 3. If what seem like coincidences and/or similarities become at all apparent, figure out if and how *Destructive, Emotion-Generated Scripting* has taken place in your client.

Step 4. Describe and explain the *Destructive, Emotion-Generated Scripting* to your client that you believe is relevant and negative.

Step 5. Help your client to recognize and *understand* the scripting and the (repeated) destructive choices and acts that your client has made and committed, respectively, as a result of these scripts.

Step 6. As simply and clearly as you can, explain and lay out the process of *Destructive, Emotion-Generated Scripting* (including the possible genetic aspects) as it relates to your client's life, beliefs, behaviors, and choices, in addition to the specific consequences that have resulted therefrom.

Step 7. After effectively completing the first 6 steps, allow some time to elapse, so that the new information can be constructively assimilated by your client, and perhaps, for the first time, objectively understood and analyzed by the client as well. Hopefully, through further discussions and analyses, the client will gain real insight and will *consciously* recognize the sources of the scripting; the processes of the scripting; the direct effects of the scripting; and the varied consequences of the scripting.

Step 8. After the client sees, understands, and appreciates his or her *Destructive, Emotion-Generated Scripting* and has its highly potent energy charges significantly dissipated, he or she is then ready to *Frisual* and begin making *Golden* and *Truthful* life choices in the area at issue.

Chapter 6

Your Killer Emotions Glossary

Destructive, Emotion-Generated Scripting: This occurs when highly potent energy charges generated by certain emotions within your *Heart-of-Hearts* continually cause or lead you to make and take the same or a similar self-defeating and/or self-sabotaging life choice and action, respectively.

Energy Charge: The energy that is generated by an emotion, impulse, urge, or compulsion that motivates and fuels you to make a certain life choice.

Emotion-Generated Triggers: Certain individuals, events, things, thoughts, goals, values, and the like that strike a deep chord within your *Heart-of-Hearts*; as a result, they elicit and generate exceptionally strong energy charges within you.

Event Visualization: A process in which you visualize yourself making a specific life choice or taking a certain action that you lock into your mind, enabling you to access, replay, and potentially follow it at *Crunch Time!*.

Frame™: An agenda-driven crafting of the life choice before you, which inevitably motivates and leads you to make a *Golden* and/or *Truthful* life choice at *Crunch Time!*.

Framing™: A process whereby you craft the life choice before you in such a way that you are inevitably led to make a *Golden/Truthful* life choice.

The Frisual™: A *Golden* and *Truthful* life-choice-making vehicle comprised of a *Frame* or set of *Frames*, and a *visual* or set of *visuals*.

General Anticipation: A process whereby you anticipate that there will be a person, thing, or event about which you do not know enough to prepare a specific, ironclad life choice during your *Prevent Offense*. Therefore, you need to be more flexible with your plans and potential choices depending upon who is or what data are presented to you at *Crunch Time!*.

Heart-of-Hearts: A metaphorical place deep inside your heart. Think of it as a combination of your heart, soul, and psyche. Your *Heart-of-Hearts* is a magical place, as it takes in energies and feelings that you perceive from the outside world; and depending upon whether these feelings are perceived by you to be positive or negative, this is how you will feel about other people; other things or events; and/or yourself. Oftentimes, what goes into your *Heart-of-Hearts* comes out in one behavioral form or another.

As positive, empowering energy charges are stored in your *Heart-of-Hearts*, you will channel these catalyzing, highly potent energy charges into your *Frames* and *visuals*, so that you are inevitably led to make a *Golden/Truthful* choice at *Crunch Time!*.

PETS or *Personal Emotional Triggers*: The people, events, things, places, or thoughts that strike a deep emotional chord within you; as a result, they trigger extremely high-voltage energy charges. It is your *PETS* that you want to incorporate into your *Frames* and *visuals* in order to overpower and thereby negate the energy charges from potentially poisonous emotions, enabling you to make a potentially sabotaging-emotion-free life choice.

Your Gold and *Your Truth* comprise *Your PETS*.

The Prevent Offense: A set of *4 Steps* specifically designed to enable you to prepare certain important data and a life choice or set of life choices in anticipation of and to be utilized at *Crunch Time!*.

Quick Frame™: An abbreviated, energy-charge-loaded *Frame* that enables you to make a *Golden* and/or *Truthful* life choice. At some point, a *Quick Frame* can generate the same high-potency energy charges as your full *Frames,* in less time and with less effort.

Quick Pic: A quick, energy-charge-loaded visual that inevitably leads you to make a *Golden* and/or *Truthful* life choice. At some point, a *Quick Pic* can generate the same high-potency energy charges as your full *visual* in less time and with less effort.

Specific Anticipation: A process that occurs during the preparation of your *Prevent Offense* when you have enough specific data about the people, things, and events involved in a future life choice, such that you can effectively prepare a specific *Golden* and/or *Truthful* life choice to make at *Crunch Time!*.

Toxic-Energy-Charge Dissipation™ *(TECD*™*)*: A process that is designed to dissipate the potency, "juice," and effectiveness of potentially poisonous energy charges that have led and can lead you to make a destructive and/or self-sabotaging life choice.

Regular-Strength TECD is used by you in connection with *The 7 Steps of Emotion Mastery* in order to dissipate the power of potentially poisonous energy charges that exist at the time you are about to make a life choice. *Extra-Strength TECD* is used in connection with emotions that are abnormally strong, either because they are deeply embedded in your *Heart-of-Hearts* (strength) or because they have existed within your *Heart-of-Hearts* for a long period of time (duration). Because the energy charges are so strong in these cases, the help of a counselor or therapist is highly recommended. The most effective point at which to engage in *Extra-Strength ECD* is during the preparation of your *Prevent Offense*, as you may well have the necessary time then to do the self-exploration required to overcome the challenges presented by these supremely potent energy charges.

Visual: One of the two components of a *Frisual*. The visualization of a certain person, event, consequence, or thing that generates such a potent energy charge in your *Heart-of-Hearts* that you are motivated and inevitably led to make a *Golden* and/or *Truthful* life choice at *Crunch Time!*.

Continue Your Emotion-Mastery Education at www.yourkilleremotions.com and www.lifechoicepsychology.com

Your Killer Emotions is devoted to enabling you to significantly enhance your life through the beneficial choices that you will make.

Two core objectives of this book are that you will continually grow as a decision-maker and evolve as a wise, understanding, compassionate, and loving person. With these goals in mind, please visit the Web site for *Your Killer Emotions* at www.yourkilleremotions.com, as well as www.lifechoicepsychology.com, for new information, insights, and stories.

Endnotes

A. Peck, Dr. M. Scott, *A Road Less Traveled* (New York: Touchstone, 1978).

B. Covey, Stephen R., *7 Habits of Highly Effective People* (New York: Fireside, 1989).

C. *White Collar*, produced by Fox Television Studios.

D. Lindner, Ken, *Crunch Time!: 8 Steps to Making the Right Life Decisions at the Right Times* (New York: Gotham Books, 2005).

E. Cowherd, Colin.

F. Peck, *op. cit*.

This book is inspired by and is a direct reflection of the brilliance of my mom, Betty Lindner. Mom, you are amazing, and I love you beyond articulation. This book is also dedicated to my dad, Jack Lindner, who is always with me and has been my teacher and inspiration by example.

I love you both as much as—if not more than—any child can possibly love his parents. Thank you, so very much, for everything that you have been and for everything that you have given to me.

This book is also dedicated to the following very special individuals and families:

To Melinda, Mary, and Tristan. I love you incredibly and endlessly. You inspire me every day! Thank you!

To Debbi and Lee Alpert, Mel Berger, the Berman family, Suzanne Bernstein, the Cammarata family, Steven Carter, Justin Chambers, Sid Clayman, Thomas Dingman, Robert Dealy, Shirley Dumpit, Liz and Michael Foster, Klaus Freundrich-Koch, Cookie and Lester Gold, the Guardado family, the Hartley family, the Havens family, the Hirsch family, the Kaplan family, Tom and Andi Karwoski, Deborah Kubiak, Dr. Jack Levin, Mike Mansel, Dr. Charles Masterson, Nena Madonia, the Mehlman family, Cheri Michelson, Jan Miller, Billy Millman, Robert Morrison, Cindy Moyneur and the Moyneur family, the Myers family, Wendy Padob, Peanut, Ricki Rest, Steve Ross, Cyndi Sarnoff-Ross, the Scheer family, the Schwartz family, the Seidlin family, the Siskind family, Garda Tan, the Tilk family, Jenny Torculas, the Young family, Pauline Youngblood, and Martine Zoller;

To my wonderful KLA staff and family: Karen Wang-Lavelle, Susan Levin, Kristin Allen, Rob Jordan, Melissa Van Fleet, Tom Ragonnet, Jill Walter, Lexi Strumor, Nick Goeringer, Eric Moreno, and Dan Foley;

To Shari Freis, who, with her warm smile, constant encouragement, and awesome skills, enables me each and every day to multitask and somehow get it all done;

To all of my treasured clients who have trusted me to help them grow;

To Clint Greenleaf, Justin Branch, Natalie Navar, Alan Grimes, Bill Crawford, Tanya Hall, Sheila Parr, Neil Gonzalez, Abby Kitten, Corrin Foster, Jonas Koffler, Steven Elizalde, Carly Willsie, Kristen Cudd, Jesse Goff, and all of the truly amazing members of the Greenleaf Book Group for all of their help, guidance, and support;

To Edward Miller for his absolutely stellar work typing, proofreading, and copy editing this book;

To Amanda Murray for all of her excellent insights as to how to best write and organize this book;

To all of my cherished broadcasting friends;

To all of my dear friends from Brooklyn Ethical Culture School, Brooklyn Poly Prep, Harvard University, and Cornell Law School;

To all of my wonderful Extreme Tennis/Paddle Tennis and tennis friends;

To Marvin, David, Jon, and Samantha Saul at Junior's Deli; and Jennifer, Elie, and Sean Jahanbigloo at Juan Juan Salon for allowing me to sit in your establishments for hours at a time and write this book;

To all of my wonderful, supportive friends whom I've not mentioned above;

And above all, to *you*, the reader. May reading this book enable you to make highly beneficial choices for the rest of your life!

—Ken

Ken Lindner, the founder of *Life-Choice Psychology*, has counseled thousands of individuals over the past thirty years and helped them to make life-enhancing personal and professional decisions. He currently owns and operates the country's premiere news and hosting representation firm, Ken Lindner and Associates, Inc. Among many of the notable individuals whose careers he has helped to develop are Matt Lauer, Lester Holt, Mario Lopez, Robin Meade, Megyn Kelly, Tom Bergeron, Shepard Smith, Sam Champion, Dr. Bruce Hensel, and Nancy O'Dell.

One of Ken's primary missions in life is to enable individuals to make well thought-out, positive life choices. He focuses on both the cognitive, as well as the all-important emotion-based, components of decision-making. By virtue of his guidance, those with whom Ken works are able to think and reason with crystal clarity and free of toxic emotions. As a result, these individuals, time after time, make life choices that reflect and effect their most highly valued goals.

Ken graduated Magna Cum Laude from Harvard University, where his honor's thesis was devoted to the science of decision-making. He later graduated from Cornell Law School, where he focused on conflict resolution.